MARC BOLAN THE LEGENDARY YEARS

MARC
BOLAN

THE LEGENDARY YEARS

JOHN & SHAN BRAMLEY

PHOTOGRAPHS BY KEITH MORRIS

SMITH GRYPHON
PUBLISHERS

DEDICATED TO OUR FRIENDS, FAMILY AND, MOST
ESPECIALLY, THE FANS.
AND TO MARC, THE MAIN MAN, FOR WHOM THE
LIGHT OF LOVE STILL BURNS BRIGHT

OFFICIAL MARC BOLAN FAN CLUB
P O Box 122, Belton, Nr Doncaster, South Yorkshire DN9 1QE

This new edition first published in 1997 by
SMITH GRYPHON LIMITED
12 Bridge Wharf
156 Caledonian Road
London N1 9UU

Originally published by Smith Gryphon in
Great Britain in a hardback edition in 1992
and in paperback in 1993

A CIP catalogue for this book is available from the British Library

ISBN 1 85685 138 9

Printed and bound in Great Britain by
Butler & Tanner Ltd. Frome

CONTENTS

ACKNOWLEDGEMENTS

In the summer of 1991 we were gathering together a list of rock personalities who had either worked with Marc, vied for a place in the charts alongside him or, quite simply, had admired him as teenagers and had been influenced enough by him to take the path to fame themselves. The interviews that were being arranged were for a new Marc Bolan television documentary planned for September 1992, the fifteenth anniversary of his death. It was while talking to Rat Scabies of the Damned that the name of Keith Morris, a well-known and respected photographer was mentioned. He suggested we should check out Keith, as he was very close to Marc and had some great photographs of him.

Keith Morris duly arrived a couple of weeks later at the editing suite where we were working in London and during a lull produced a well-worn mock-up of a book he and Marc had planned in 1972. On looking through the pages memories were stirred, images of Marc in moods never publicly seen before. We were holding a photographic time-capsule, one that we felt should not and could not be lost for ever to the fans of Marc Bolan who, to this day, still idolize him. For this we would like to thank Keith Morris from the bottom of our hearts.

We would like to say thank you to Robert Smith, our publisher, who got himself into this venture over lunch one day and who we feel has a deep understanding of fan-star relationships. To Helen Armitage for editing and teaching us a few new words – none of which we shall probably ever use again! To Vicki, Lorna and Lesley at ILS. To James Harmon and Rosemary Bloom for having allowed our dream to remain a reality. To Bill Legend and Mickey Finn of T.Rex who have both become good friends and have given us some great laughs and memories over the years. To 'Uncle' David Platz, to whom we owe so much from the early days. We now realize why Marc Bolan and June Feld addressed David affectionately as 'Uncle' – his kindness, understanding and belief have allowed us to mature in confidence.

During the years following the death of Marc Bolan, we have met, been influenced, befriended and even hated by fans left behind, such is the passion associated with the name Marc Bolan. There are a few fans we would like to acknowledge here because, in their own ways, they have all contributed to ensuring

the name of Marc Bolan lives on in people's hearts and minds: Paul Sinclair, who produced, we believe, the first true Bolan fanzine, *Cosmic Dancer*; Pete Old for *T.Rex Times*; Dave and Dave of the T.Rex Appreciation Society, the first attempt to bring together Marc's stunned fans after his death; the Silver Surfer, Dave Williams, who got little reward for his hard work on a book to inspire any Bolan fan who wants to know everything about Marc Bolan; John and Joan Reagan, whose donation of a track helped to launch us on the record-company trail; John Willans and Caron Thomas, who, at the eleventh hour, helped us with some American information; and Kevin Knowles. A sincere tanx to them all.

There are many friends who are special, and as such we would like to mention them here: Jacki and Dale Oades, who helped us to get the petty stupidity of others out of our systems by seeing everything from a different perspective; to Lynn and Dave Temperton, who helped by taking some of the pressure off us in earlier times; to Shan's best friend, Jacqui Oakley, from the seventies – Scunthorpe's only T.Rex fans, or so it seemed at the time!; to Dave Sidwells, John's oldest friend, who, like John, remembers the Empire Pool with pride, not forgetting Gerry, Dave's wife, who has to stay awake when the old timers get together; to Diane Lobbett, John's sister, and her husband, Gary, who tolerate us, but fail to understand what Marc Bolan means to us, even now, all these years later; to Shan's mum and dad, Martha and Ernie Leaning, for always being ready to look after things; to June Feld (Bolan), Marc Bolan's widow, who over the years has become a very special friend, as well as a consistent driving force behind all our efforts; to Steve Currie, a nicer bass player you would never meet, who died in Portugal in 1981 in a car crash, of all things; and finally to Emma, Edward, Thomas, Rebecca, Jessica, Louis, Carly, Kristofer, Cara . . . the future.

The authors and publisher would like to acknowledge the contributions from articles by Danny Holloway (*New Musical Express*), Derek Boltwood (*Record Mirror*), Charles Shaar Murray (*New Musical Express*), Steve Peacock (*Sounds*), Val Mabbs (*Record Mirror*), Nick Logan (*Sounds*), Chris Welch (*Melody Maker*); and to Wizard (Bahamas) Ltd for the use of two lines from 'Children of the Revolution' reproduced on p. 58.

PREFACE

An all encompassing historical work on the life of Marc Bolan would be a huge undertaking. To refer to all the people who have been involved with him would have meant a much longer quest than we had time available to write this book and indeed would have sent us across the globe. To have attempted to pad it out with speculation is something that neither of us wanted to do; unfortunately that's been done before and has not helped best serve any interests.

There are periods in Marc's career that are vague, to say the least, and we apologize for any omissions that may become apparent on publication. That said, we believe that we have been factual and have taken a giant step in providing a fresh look at the Marc Bolan whom many of us were fortunate to know, admire and now sadly miss. If we have served Marc in whetting the appetite of fans, old and new, for even greater knowledge, then we shall feel content that we have achieved something.

INTRODUCTION

John Bramley Many books have been written in the past about the life and career of Marc Bolan, each written in its own special way. This book, too, is written in our own special way. We were, as teenagers, brought up through those oh-so-awkward years with Marc Bolan very much a part of our lives. The memories are very dear and yet at times intense with the pain and anger that you experience when you feel that an artist belongs to you and your fellow followers alone. The euphoria of seeing Marc in concert will stay with me for the remainder of my days. I remember seeing him at Bristol and Cardiff in the weeks following the release of 'Ride a White Swan'. Great gigs. I remember seeing him again at Bristol in May 1971 and on the *Electric Warrior* tour at Leicester's De Montfort Hall.

Life as a fan was getting to be a mite dangerous! My greatest experience was being at the Wembley Empire Pool the day Marc was crowned and I can remember only three things about that memorable day: sheer terror when Marc came on stage and I was shoved forward by a mass of bodies; leaving the stadium soaked with sweat; and having a headache that stayed with me for days.

But I also remember the not-so-good times. When Marc seemingly turned his back on us in England – after all we had done for him! When I sat, unashamedly, and cried when my sister taunted me while Marc staggered through 'Teenage Dream' on *Top of the Pops*. Such naivety was all part of growing up, I suppose, and with hindsight I realize that Marc had another life and owed us nothing. In fact it was when Marc died that I realized that it was I who owed Marc everything.

Shan Bramley My introduction to Marc was through the radio when I heard 'Ride a White Swan' for the first time. Wow!! The first single I could afford to purchase was not until the middle of 1971 when 'Get It On' started my Bolan record collection.

My one big regret that will live with me for the rest of my days is that, unlike John, I never got the chance to see Marc live in concert – I was never to experience that feeling of belonging, of being able to reach out and touch him. He did, however, touch my life in other ways I shall never forget. His cheeky smile will be with me for ever.

Keith Morris: a recollection During the psychedelic flower-power days of the sixties, Keith Morris was a photographer whose pictures graced the pages of the underground magazine of the day, *Oz*. Although *Oz* has ceased publication long since, such is the magazine's continued cult status that in 1992 a complete mint set of *Oz* was seen at auction with a price tag of £1800.

Keith Morris and Marc Bolan knew each other casually for some years. Between 1967 and 1970, while Tyrannosaurus Rex were weaving magical spells on small but dedicated audiences, through the lens of his camera Keith Morris was observing the growth of a great many underground and folky musicians and artists, including Martin Carthy, Nick Drake, Mighty Baby, the Incredible String Band, the UK blues band Ainslee Dunbar Retaliation – Dunbar later became drummer with Frank Zappa & the Mothers of Invention – and, of course, Marc Bolan. These musicians, and a great many more, were all sessioned by Keith. He also covered live gigs: the Rolling Stones, Cream and the Nice, in its later incarnation as the excellent Emerson, Lake and Palmer.

Keith had photographed Tyrannosaurus Rex in concert on a few occasions, but it was off stage that he was to get his first good look at Bolan, and he remembers very clearly his thoughts when he finally got to meet him at a party hosted by a mutual friend:

'"Ooh, I'd love to get you in front of a camera!" He was bopping Elfman straight out of Gandolf's garden – he was a natural.'

Quite incredibly, it was not until the change to T.Rex in 1970 at the beginning of their most successful era that Keith was able finally to focus his lens on the new rock sensation. It was as a result of an album sleeve he had shot for another band that Keith received a phone call from Tony Secunda, Marc's business adviser. Keith explains:

'Marc and Tony had seen a Mighty Baby album sleeve that I had sessioned a couple of years before. They liked it, so Tony Secunda phoned and invited me to do a studio shoot with Messrs Bolan and Finn.' Keith was not entirely sure about it all as Marc was a 'teeny idol' in the making and he himself was much more into the serious side of music. But the shoot was booked anyway and Marc arrived on time, though Mickey was late – apparently quite a regular Finn occurrence. Keith

recalls the introduction:

'Marc and I sat and drank a whole bottle of this strange herb liqueur called Herbitas; it tasted a bit minty and extremely alcoholic. By the time Mickey Finn arrived we were well relaxed – we really clicked. The session was a great success and the fun shows through – great days!'

Keith Morris soon found himself part of the team. Over the next nine or ten months he was photographing Marc Bolan non-stop.

'At one point I was taking pictures four days a week,' Keith recalls, staggered by the memory of it all. 'I remember my first live shoot with Marc at the Gliderdrome in Boston, Lincolnshire, in the July of 1971. I went on to the stage to check out a couple of places I had earmarked for possible shots, when suddenly a tremendous roar filled my ears as the kids thought I was a member of the band. I turned around to face them, looking into the lights, and the sight was awesome. Stretching away into the distance was this sea of faces and outstretched hands, many holding aloft pictures of Marc Bolan's face. Just like the archive footage you see of the Nazi Nuremberg rallies of the 1930s, truly amazing.'

By the late summer of 1972, Keith felt it was time to start concentrating on other projects: 'There were people gathering around Marc; the personal contact was getting to be less. Marc was by now a huge rock star. He had a great deal to watch over and at times I'm sure things got out of hand. I took more pictures of Marc at the end of the year and throughout the remainder of his career I did the occasional shoot, but the period of '71 and '72? They were crazy, crazy days.'

.   .   .

'My Bolan pix had lain untouched for nearly twenty years. Then one day, I got a call from John and Shan asking if I'd take part in a series of interviews they were doing with people who had known, and worked with Marc. As it was being filmed to go with a TV special they were producing, they asked me if I would print up a few pix to edit in behind my talking head. However, being basically lazy I just took along the mock-up of a book Marc and I had planned many years before. When they saw it they loved it and both said they felt the pictures really should be published.

'This wasn't the first time somebody had said this sort of thing, yet always for the wrong avaricious reasons, but I decided to talk about it with them. During the day we discussed how best to update the presentation of what was, after all, a twenty-year-old mock-up, and I began to realize that I only really wanted to go ahead if they, John and Shan, were heavily involved in writing and co-ordinating the whole thing. I had three reasons for this: firstly, their lifelong love for, and dedication to, Marc and his music. Secondly, their unique and encyclopaedic knowledge of the Bolan years and, thirdly, their concern with getting it right more than in making a few quick beans . . . and thus it came to pass that I spent Christmas of '91 in a dark room.'

1 · Strange Orchestras

Marc Bolan's introduction to rock 'n' roll came as the result of a fortunate error by his father, Simeon Feld. In 1955, when Marc was eight, to encourage his son's early interest in music he had just bought him a record player and his first ever single, 'The Ballad of Davey Crockett', by the American singer, Bill Hayes. On one of Simeon's record-hunting trips down London's Petticoat Lane market, he thought he had found a new album by Hayes, which he presented proudly to his son. As it spun on the record player, Marc discovered his father's error, and the new and exciting sounds from America of Bill Haley and the Comets. He was soon off on a musical voyage of discovery: Elvis Presley, Buddy Holly, Little Richard and Eddie Cochran. Other early influences were closer to home. Britain was in the grip of Lonnie Donegan and skiffle music and it was easy to join in: any young skiffle freak could set themselves up as a skiffle band with the aid of a tea chest and their mother's washboard.

Marc's parents, Phyllis and Simeon Feld, must take a great deal of the credit for encouraging the emergence of Marc as a young musician. He was born Mark Feld on 30 September 1947 in Hackney General Hospital, East London, into a Jewish family that, although not poor, were by no means wealthy. Despite limited financial resources, the family did their best, though, to feed Marc's continual interest in music. Having first watched with amazement as he built himself a very rough guitar, on which he learnt the basic chords, his parents paid the then huge amount of £16.00 for his first proper musical instrument. Marc himself paid his own way in his pursuit of records and music in general by helping his mother on her fruit stall in Soho's Berwick Street market, and by working part time around the corner at a coffee bar known as the 2i's. Situated in Old Compton Street in the heart of London's West End, this was where Marc was able to earn £2.00 serving coffee at weekends.

It was here at the 2i's, where Marc heard his first skiffle music, that Tommy Steele was discovered and Cliff Richard and the Shadows made their début. Of the 2i's Marc was later to say: 'I auditioned there myself one day, but they turned me down,' supposedly on the same day as another young hopeful, Harry Webb, soon to find fame as Cliff Richard.

Marc's schooling had been basic. From Northwold Primary through to Hill Croft in Wimbledon, south London where his parents had moved from north London's Stamford Hill when he was fourteen, he had found education a bore. He had little interest in the subjects taught at school, which was through no lack of intelligence, and due rather to an incredibly overactive and creative mind that was always preoccupied with ideas, especially those of the poets and storytellers which were available to him.

In an attempt to find a creative outlet for himself, while at William Wordsworth School he had joined his first band Susie & the Hoola Hoops. The band's lead singer was Helen Shapiro, who was to become one of those musical discoveries that happen from time to time when within a few months she had left the Hoola Hoops to release a string of pop-chart hits during 1961 and 1962: 'Don't Treat Me Like a Child', 'Tell Me What He Said', plus her two singles chart number ones, 'You Don't Know' and 'Walkin' Back to Happiness'.

Marc himself had joined the band playing tea-chest bass, a far cry from his first love, the guitar. Yet what more of an incentive could there have been for a young man than to see one of his own making hit singles? Later he was quoted as remembering that he did not relate to Shapiro's success at all and had found it difficult to believe. Aware of his own unfulfilled desires, it was to him a shimmering mirage.

Shortly after leaving school – from where, in fact, he was expelled for bad behaviour – Marc got involved with the contemporary mod scene, which had evolved as an extension of the fifties' beatniks and was concerned with modern jazz and philosophy, amphetamines and John Lee Hooker. As a young dude about town, he actually featured in a large glossy magazine, *Town*, which was doing a pictorial feature on mod fashions. The photographs were taken by Don McCullin, now the famous war photographer, and are acknowledged as the first photographs to appear in print of Marc. *Town* is recognized as the forerunner to the outbreak of men's magazines in the 1980s and 1990s, such as *GQ* and *For Him*. It was a serious publication and in the September 1962 issue carried an article by Peter Barnsley about the mods under the heading 'Faces Without Shadows', an apparent reference to the youthful faces at the forefront of the new scene. It gives an

interesting insight into the then undiscovered Bolan: *F**eld is fifteen years old, and still at school. His family has just moved from Stamford Hill to a pre-fab out in Wimbledon. Of this he does not approve. The queues of Teds outside the cinemas in Wimbledon look just like a contest for the worst haircut, he says. At least the boys of old Stamford Hill dress sharply, and who would want a new, clean house if it is in unsympathetic surroundings? None the less cleanliness is of vital importance to him. Shining with soap and health, he is apparently tireless and often goes for days on end without any sleep; there is never a trace of fatigue or boredom in his face.*

What is the point of all this energy and all the soap and water? Where is the goal towards which he is obviously running as fast as his impeccably shod feet can carry him? It is nowhere.

Marc proceeds obviously to boast to Barnsley: *I**'ve got ten suits, eight sports jackets, fifteen pairs of slacks, thirty to thirty-five good shirts, about twenty jumpers, three leather jackets, two suede jackets, five or six pairs of shoes and thirty exceptionally good ties.... Three years ago we used to go round on Scooters in Levis and leather jackets.*

Barnsley comments, 'But you would have been twelve years old!'

'That's right,' responds Marc. It was not to be the last time that Marc was capable of the most outrageous claims.

In August 1967, the *Observer* colour supplement examined the mod trend. Marc was featured again, even though, by this time as a nineteen year old, he had moved on and was working in the music business himself as Tyrannosaurus Rex.

'I thought those Mods were just fantastic. I used to go home and literally pray to become a Mod.'

Bolan did some modelling work for the menswear chain of John Temple, who were apparently unimpressed or too ready to use new faces as he was not used by them again. There are also reports that he modelled for mail-order catalogues, such as Freemans and Littlewoods, but we have never seen any evidence of this.

However, it was following his brief career as a model that Marc decided to

follow the music trail more closely. He started as a folk singer by name of Toby Tyler and found that the folk-music circuit suited him, with only his guitar for company. At the time he had no one else with whom to form any kind of musical partnership. This was when the first of many managers discovered him.

Allan Warren was an actor who saw in Marc a 'baby-faced Cliff Richard' and the agreement was that if Toby should become successful, Allan Warren would manage his affairs. Acetates were recorded and Marc, as Toby Tyler, sang the Betty Everett song 'You're No Good' for a major record company test. Sadly, he failed to impress them and Toby Tyler and Allan Warren parted company soon afterwards. In recent years two Toby Tyler acetates have resurfaced – 'The Road I'm on, Gloria' and a cover of the Bob Dylan classic 'Blowin' in the Wind' – the latter purchased by a print and design company for £4000.

. . .

It was a time of conscious change for Marc. He had decided to concentrate on learning how to write songs and play the guitar and with that in mind he dropped the Toby Tyler name. Sheer doggedness and determination to succeed led him to be shown the door at most of the major record companies in London. Yet, his fortunes seemed to change for the better when he met up with Jim Economedies, a producer with Decca Records, with whom he finally recorded his first single 'The Wizard'.

At this time, in 1965, there was another change that initially had little to do with Marc. On delivery of the white label advance copy of the new single Mac noticed that the artiste's name was written as Mark Bowland. When he asked for an explanation, Decca simply advised Marc that Mark Feld did not look good. It must be remembered that these were the days when many artists did not have a say in their own destiny and subsequently says much for the attitude of the fresh-faced Bolan that he insisted on having some input on his name change and consequent image. He persuaded them as a result to change the letter K in his christian name to a C and remove the W and D from his surname: Marc Bolan had arrived.

Between the years of 1965 when 'The Wizard' was released and September of

1967 when Marc met up with Steve Took to form Tyrannosaurus Rex there was little to shout about. 'The Wizard' was a flop, despite his appearance on the pop-hits music show, *Ready Steady Go!* To say his slot there was a disaster would be an understatement, as the band backing Marc missed the intro and played too fast and out of key. This was an introduction to life dependent on others and was one that Marc could have done well without. His follow-up single 'The Third Degree' released in June 1966 did little better than 'The Wizard' and Decca decided to part company with him. It was then that Marc met his first heavyweight manager in the form of Simon Napier Bell.

Napier Bell had managed the Yardbirds in the sixties and clearly recalls his first introduction to Marc:

'Somehow he got hold of my home telephone number and simply called me up. "I'm a singer and I am going to be the biggest rock star ever, so I need a good manager." ' Simon suggested that Marc should send a tape to his office, but, with a great deal of nerve, Marc told Napier Bell that as he was quite close to his house and he could drop in with the tape. A short while later there was Marc on Simon's doorstep, with a huge smile and a guitar around his neck. A personal appearance by an aspiring musician was usually the thing that Simon hated most; there was nothing worse than listening to someone without knowing how or when to stop them. But, he let Marc right into his home – having seen instant evidence of his panache and star quality.

Marc sang to him for about fifty minutes and in the end Napier Bell stopped him, not because he hated what he heard, but simply because he had to call a studio and book a session. At eight o'clock that evening Marc started his performance again and when listening to him again the following day Napier thought he sounded even better. He was more than pleased and quite convinced that one of the songs could be a hit single.

'Hippy Gumbo' was produced by Simon and included a string section. With it, Marc Bolan was back on the single release sheets and reviewed by one music paper as 'a crazed mixture of an incredibly bad negro blues singer and Larry the Lamb'. They were obviously not impressed and, even without such helpful reviews, the single flopped.

It was after this débâcle that Simon Napier Bell suggested that Marc should join another of Simon's bands, John's Children. Reportedly, Simon decided to place Marc with them because he did not know what else to do with him, but Marc told a different story when he was interviewed several years later by Danny Holloway of the *New Musical Express*.

'John's Children were visually interesting but it was felt that they needed a kind of Pete Townsend, so they picked on me.' Both versions seem possible, but the real reasons and the initial idea came from another source.

In the Simon Napier Bell and Chris Welch biography, *Marc Bolan: Born to Boogie*, a much more reasonable explanation of Marc's joining the band is given. It would seem that the credit goes to Kit Lambert, then the manager of the Who, who had just formed his own record label, Track Records. The first two acts signed to Track were Jimi Hendrix and John's Children and Lambert insisted that part of the package with Simon was the inclusion of Marc Bolan on guitar. Having a record deal on the same label as Jimi Hendrix was exactly the kind of kick Bolan liked as Hendrix was one of his new heroes.

John's Children were supposedly the first of the psychedelic acts of the sixties, and it was really their on-stage antics more than anything else that got them noticed. They did have minor hits but their main claim to fame is the title of a faked live album they recorded in 1966. *Orgasm*, when advertised in America, was banned, mainly because the girl on the front cover appeared to be having exactly that! In the well-documented book, *John's Children* by Dave Thompson, the band's vocalist, Andy Ellison reflects on their first meeting with Marc at Simon Napier Bell's flat:

'This little guy came walking in with a copy of *Blonde On Blonde*. We spent the rest of the evening sitting around listening to that and didn't see Marc again until he turned up one evening at the club.' In the same book, Chris Townson, drummer with John's Children, also recalled how *M*arc, before joining John's Children in March, had never played an electric guitar. His first one was a really stodgy old Gibson SG, which Simon bought from Trevor White of the A-Jaes. He played it incredibly loudly. His first rehearsal with us was deafening, even by our

standards! I think the band actually got worse when Marc first joined, because all he did was stand there and make this muddy blurge. It really was a horrible noise.

Track Records first John's Children release was the Bolan-penned 'Desdemona'. It was banned from airplay by the BBC reportedly for the mention of the word 'nude' and the line 'Lift up your skirts and fly'. While appreciating that Marc was seen to be in a band of dubious morals, in comparison with the clean-cut image of such bands as Herman's Hermits and the Beatles, these were hardly shocking lyrics. Indeed, Marc was to maintain that the line was a reference to Desdemona, a witch sitting across her broom before flying off. Wherever the truth may lie, the moral of this incident is to consider the quality of mind of those who made these censorious decisions. Without the backing of airplay, the single, although a minor hit, failed.

It was the projected single 'Midsummer's Night Scene' that Marc was later to blame for him leaving John's Children. His version of his departure was that the band, aided and abetted by Simon Napier Bell's production, 'messed up' the song. The band, supported by Napier Bell's own recollections, would indicate otherwise. Andy Ellison claims that if Marc had been unhappy with the production of the single and his role in the band, he never let on to the rest of them about it. Ellison felt that the deeper and more real problem was that Marc felt his songs were much lighter in content than John's Children were treating them. Whatever, it was then that Napier Bell was approached by Marc and told that he wanted to start a band of his own. All the signs indicated that Bolan would leave and the single was withdrawn by Track Records for reasons that are unclear, even today.

The advertisement, when placed in *International Times*, once again showed Bolan's confidence, or perhaps even his overconfidence. His band was named in the advert as Tyrannosaurus Rex, the name given to the largest animal ever to walk this earth. Did Bolan plan the largest band ever to play on this earth? In any case, at the beginning, like the creature itself, Marc's new band nearly became extinct, after the very first gig.

At the same time as placing the advertisement, Bolan had booked a gig at the Electric Garden in London's Covent Garden. He chose three people for his new band, one of them was Steve Peregrine Took, named after the character from the J. R. R. Tolkien books *The Hobbit* and *The Lord of the Rings*. It is interesting to

note that Tolkien's books were heavily to influence early Tyrannosaurus Rex material and, in general, the books were not unlike a Bible to the hippies of the sixties. Even the Electric Garden itself changed its name later on to Middle Earth, another Tolkien creation.

In an article some years later in October 1972 by Charles Shaar Murray in *New Musical Express* entitled 'Steve Took: From Bolan boogie to gutter rock', Steve Took describes his first meeting with Marc Bolan: *I met Nalob Cram [as he chose to refer to Marc Bolan!] through* International Times, *which I always read, which was something about flower pots, cosmic dancers and something like that – something to do with drugs – and we met and had this band together, and I had a double drum kit then, and he'd got this guitarist together, and a bass player and we rehearsed for a while.*

Marc, it would appear, wanted to commit suicide with his new band. With little or no rehearsal, Tyrannosaurus Rex appeared at the Electric Garden and were promptly booed off stage – not very good for Marc's ego at all. It certainly was a mismatch, though, as the other two musicians were only with Marc for such a little time, the length of gig itself, that no one even knows their names. Steve Took elaborates further in Murray's *NME* piece: *We did one gig at the Electric Garden, which used to be Middle Earth, and the lead guitarist went mad.*

He started knocking my drum kit about, knocking my cymbals over, thought he was Pete Townsend. It was Pete Townsend, you know! After that we decided that we couldn't work with these other two cats.

This fiasco occurred at the same time as Marc 'lost' all his electric equipment, forcing him to turn acoustic. Once again, conflicting accounts explain the unfortunate state of affairs. Bolan's version, a simple yet traumatic one, was that when he quit John's Children, Track took back all the equipment. For his part, Simon Napier Bell says that the equipment got lost in Germany after the band's tour with the Who. Whatever the truth, Bolan and Took became an acoustic duo, and the first Tyrannosaurus Rex band was born.

.   .   .

The rocky road to musical stardom and acclaim was difficult to say the very least. Marc and Steve faced mounting debts and one of the casualties of this was Steve's drum kit, sold to raise funds to pay them off. As Took told Charles Shaar Murray: *I sold my drum kit and got some bongos, and that was that.*

I used to play flutes and penny whistles, anything just to get a boogie going. I had bongos, I had a miniature drum kit, bass, gong and pixiephone.... Well, I was falling around Harrods one day, as is my wont, in the toys section, and I saw this little thing with 'Pixiephone' written on the side.... It's really like a little kid's xylophone. So I bought the first model ... and then I progressed to the full double sharps and flat chromium-plated model.

With no electric guitars and no drum kit, initiative was the order of the day. Fortunately, it was at this time that Marc got his major slice of luck in the personage of John Peel, who became a staunch ally.

Peel has been the key to success for many acts over the years – from Adam and the Ants through the Smiths to Stiff Little Fingers – and it comes as no great surprise to find him entwined with the fortunes of Tyrannosaurus Rex. Marc sent Peel an acetate and tape of material he had recorded either on his own or with Steve Took and Peel's support of Marc began when he played 'Hippy Gumbo' some two years or so after its first release on his Radio Caroline show, *Perfumed Garden*. Peel had been impressed enough to give them airplay; after all, it was possible to get away with playing material from innovative new bands on pirate radio that commercial stations would ignore: that was half the fun.

John Peel was quoted in Essex Music's *Marc Bolan: a Tribute*, published in 1978, as having this to say about Marc: 'I liked him as a human being and I liked his music. From that time on, whenever I had a gig anywhere, I would ask Marc and Steve to go along and play.'

And the reactions to the acoustic duo? 'Often the people who were running the gig were not terribly pleased about it, because they didn't like people sitting on the stage banging children's instruments and singing in a bizzare manner.' Tyrannosaurus Rex gigged at the renamed Middle Earth in Convent Garden as support to John Peel and were invited back, again and again. 'I was billed over

them,' says Peel, 'then it all started to change. They were Tyrannosaurus Rex introduced by John Peel, which, of course, is the way it should have been.'

By the time Tyrannosaurus Rex were getting up a small but welcome head of steam, Marc was again on the lookout for new management. This was when he appeared at Blackhill Enterprises, Pink Floyd's management company, where the encounter was not especially fruitful, except that it was there that he came to meet June Childe. She explains how: *M*arc *came to see Peter Jenner because he, along with Andrew King, managed Floyd and he adored Syd Barrett. Marc felt that 'If Syd's there I want to be there too.'*

I looked up and there was this tiny, scruffy little thing, in what turned out to be his mother's flying boots, an old school blazer, with the elbows all worn out, a very thin silk scarf and greased back hair, with a sort of frizzy bit at the front.

'I've come to see Peter Jenner,' were his first words to me. I buzzed through and told Peter that somebody called Marc Bolan was here to see him and in Marc toddled. I was sitting there typing when I had this incredible feeling in my head, almost like static electricity; then it was gone and I continued typing.

Marc re-emerged some time later and I made him a cup of tea, and we talked and talked and talked. Suddenly he said, 'Oh, I must go,' and off he went, back to Wimbledon.

June carried on with her life for all of two hours when, 'The phone rang. Marc was on the line, asking urgently, "Could you come over? I have to speak to you."' June assumed that this request had something to do with the meeting he had had earlier with Peter Jenner and with Peter's okay took the Bentley owned by Pink Floyd to drive over to Wimbledon. *I remember it was a beautiful summer day. When Marc opened the door, that same static electric buzz came into my head. Marc just looked at me and said, 'Would you like some muesli?' and I remember my stunned breathless response of 'Oh, yes, please.'*

We sat out on this piece of grass, eating muesli and talking. Then Marc said, 'I've got something for you', and he reached inside his pocket and pulled out this folded piece of paper. When I opened it there was the most beautiful love poem. I

looked at him and he said, 'I'm in love with you' and I said, 'Oh, well, all right.' I was quite speechless but I knew it was right.

Marc and June spent that and the next four nights sleeping in June's van on Wimbledon Common, until they found a bedsit in Bleinheim Crescent. It was to prove an uncommonly close and fruitful alliance that was to last for years.

If his personal life had taken a turn for the better, Marc was beginning to see signs of improvement with his music and to find a genuine following at last. Tyrannosaurus Rex played colleges as well as all the open air festivals then so popular and the duo appeared at the first free Hyde Park festival in 1968. These years saw the full bloom of flower power and the hippy movement, with which Steve Took was more heavily involved than Marc. Took was later to say that Marc was, for a while at least, a good hippy. They would sit around for hours discussing how the world needed changing and while Took felt he wanted to get more into this, Marc had other ideas that evolved as they became more popular. The underground movement was no longer a priority for him.

Very much a unit, but still managerless, Bolan and Took continued gigging and one evening, during the autumn of 1967, were playing at the UFO club in London's Tottenham Court Road. As it turned out, fate had chosen this night to introduce Tony Visconti to Marc's music, which was to prove the most important musical introduction of his career.

Visconti was born in Brooklyn, New York in 1944. His early aspirations were as a musician, not in rock 'n' roll, in which he lost interest with the demise of such greats as Buddy Holly and Chuck Berry, but in jazz. Visconti married young and with his wife formed a duo called Tony and Sigrid; they had a recording contract with RCA with whom they cut three singles. Visconti wrote his own material and recorded a great deal at home and it was his boss Howie Richmond at the Richmond Organization who was to suggest to him that his future lay in record producing. At this time, fortuitously, the Richmond family owned a sister company in England called Essex Music. Tony Visconti was therefore to meet up with Denny Cordell, who worked for Essex in England, when Denny invited him over to discuss the possibility of working together. Cordell had been searching for an American producer to consolidate his love for American sounds.

By the time he got his first look at Marc Bolan at UFO, Tony had worked in Denny Cordell's Essex studio with Joe Cocker, Procol Harum and the Move, with all of whom he had produced hit singles and albums. That evening at the club, Visconti found himself among a couple of hundred people, silent and mesmerized, listening to a strange little pixie-type, who sat cross-legged on stage with a beatnik partner playing children's musical pipes and banging bongos. Intrigued and keen to talk business, Tony approached Steve Took after the gig and started to introduce himself.

'Man I'm too bummed out to talk to you. See him, he's the one who does the business,' Took replied. In fact, Tony Visconti had approached Steve first because he found Marc too intimidating. His initial judgement had been correct and when he did as Steve suggested, Marc was almost dismissive as Tony introduced himself. After all, Marc enthused, Tony was the seventh producer by whom he had been approached in the past few weeks and, didn't he know, even John Lennon wanted to work with him.

'Leave me your number anyway,' was Bolan's curt reply.

Whether Visconti was discouraged or not by Marc's response, he was mightily pleased when Marc phoned him the following day at Essex Music and asked if he could come and play to him. Within an hour, Marc turned up with Steve and they performed the entire set from the previous night's gig, on the floor of Denny Cordell's office. Cordell was confounded, but sufficiently impressed to agree to the signing of Tyrannosaurus Rex 'as our "token" underground group'. So it was that with Regal Zonophone, the record label owned by Essex Music and distributed by the powerful EMI, the first album and single 'Deborah' were to be recorded for around £400.

Released on 19 April 1968, the début single took many people by surprise with the driving rhythm of the acoustic guitar and Marc's much stronger vocals. It did quite well in the charts, registering a healthy thirty-four in the recognized British Top Forty published weekly by the BBC. The flip side 'Childstar' was a track taken from the first Tyrannosaurus Rex album *My People Were Fair and Had Sky in Their Hair But Now They're Content to Wear Stars on Their Brows*, released later on 7 July.

Tyrannosaurus Rex were folky more than anything else in the early days and the first album had a charm and simplicity of its own. The Tolkien influences were very strong and the elfs, dwarfs, unicorns and dragons were a main characteristic over the next couple of years. Tony Visconti had his own feelings about the first album he produced for the band. In *The Record Producers*, written by John Tobler and Stuart Grundy, he had this to say about the album and his favourite tracks from it:

I've still got lots of favourites, but the song I like most is an adorable little track called 'Strange Orchestras'. We only had four days completely to make that album, and whereas the other tracks were done quite quickly and frantically, and with the minimum of overdubs, 'Strange Orchestras' was our only attempt at doing something slick, where you have these little surprising sounds appearing now and then. It always conjures up for me an image of a tiny elfin orchestra, little people playing tiny little instruments. There are more beautiful songs on the album, like 'Afghan Woman' and the title track, but I still get a thrill listening to 'Strange Orchestras' on headphones.

The album appealed to a growing army of fans, mainly hippies and arty types. Yet although it reached a respectable fifteen in the English charts, Tyrannosaurus Rex did not have any Top Twenty hit singles over the next two and a half years. This was possibly due to the fact that the average hippy fan would not be caught dead buying singles. These purchasing trends were also coloured by economics, with albums being much better value than singles and easily within reach of the average punter. When the hits started several years later the situation was the reverse as youngsters bought singles and could not afford the albums.

Tyrannosaurus Rex found their gigs were getting more popular and they started performing outside of London. Between the release of the single and first album, in the early summer of 1968 they visited Scotland during a seven-day tour, starting at Inverness and moving on a daily basis to Motherwell, Dundee and Glasgow, to finish in Edinburgh on 26 May.

Their new-found success made a big difference to life in general. One minute June and Marc had put Marc's guitar in hock to find the rent of £3.8s.6d (£3.42$\frac{1}{2}$) a week and the next Tyrannosaurus Rex were getting £20.00 a gig. More success

was to follow. On 6 July, Tyrannosaurus Rex appeared at the Woburn Abbey Festival in Bedfordshire among the contemporary pop-music elite of Family, Donovan, and the Jimi Hendrix Experience. At another free festival in Hyde Park, alongside acts such as Pink Floyd, Roy Harper and Jethro Tull, Tyrannosaurus Rex played to over 8000 fans. Within two months of these gigs and the release of the first album, the band were able to negotiate fees of over £100 a night.

As 1968 progressed into late summer, on 23 August a follow-up single 'One Inch Rock' was released, with a flip-side title of 'Salamanda Palaganda' from a newly completed album not yet released. The single broke into the UK Top Thirty, albeit only peaking at twenty-eight, yet giving Marc his first taste of minor chart success. People were beginning to take notice of Tyrannosaurus Rex, slowly, but surely. This was evident when, on 2 October, Marc undertook his first full tour as Tyrannosaurus Rex. They took in eight dates, kicking off at Leytonstone in Essex at the Red Lion pub and moving on to Nottingham (9th), Blackburn (11th), Birmingham (14th), Sheffield (15th), Southampton (20th), Dunstaple (29th) and finally Hull on the 30th at the end of the month. Midway through this tour their second album was released with a title equally as long as the first, called *Prophets, Seers and Sages, The Angel of the Ages*. Its release, on 14 October was met mainly with good reviews as the enchanting voice of Bolan mystified many, yet left the listener wanting to know and hear more. Quite incredibly it did not chart. For reasons still not understood, the album did not live up to Bolan's expectations from the gathering momentum of popular support, which continued regardless. Like a fairylit juggernaut that has built up speed on the main highway, Tyrannosaurus Rex were unstoppably on the road to fame and stardom.

2 · Changes

January 1969 opened with the release of 'Pewter Suitor' on the fourteenth. This, their third single, was a flop, failing to register at all on the best-selling singles listings. Bolan was perplexed but not demoralized as the failure of the single did not cross over to the gigs. Tyrannosaurus Rex were increasingly in demand and Marc, now more eager than ever to reach a growing legion of converts, was bitten by the travelling bug. Finally his destiny was beginning to unfold: he knew he had to conquer the United Kingdom and Europe, before attempting the richer harvests of the United States.

June Childe had now left Blackhill and increasingly took care of all Marc's business dealings, even to the extent of chauffeuring him to all the gigs. Of June, Danae Brooks, a reporter for the London *Evening News* was later to say, 'She is independent, energetic and practically creative. It was her dynamism coupled with Marc's musicianship and ability to write which enabled him to achieve the thing he most wanted – stardom.'

During February 1969 Tyrannosaurus Rex performed just four gigs, appearing first at the Birmingham Town Hall on the 15th, followed by Fairfield Hall in Croydon on the 16th, Manchester Free Trade Hall on the 22nd and Bristol Colston Hall on the 23rd. March continued in the same vein, with Marc and Steve appearing at the Philharmonic Hall in Liverpool on the 1st, ending their tour at the Dome, in Brighton, on the 8th.

Just prior to the release of the third album *Unicorn* in May 1969, an article by Derek Boltwood appeared in *Record Mirror* under the heading 'From the Underworld'. It was a piece about underground groups, but Boltwood appears to have had visionary powers, both in recognizing the possible superstar who played before him and in being, we believe, the first person to abbreviate the name Tyrannosaurus Rex to T.Rex. Was it genius or was it just laziness, or lack of copy space? Here it is, anyway: *The audience is not exactly hostile or aggressive but it certainly doesn't know quite what to expect. The reception they give is not exactly cold and not exactly hot. Plenty of polite noise and lukewarm clapping that says: 'We've heard of you and heard your albums, now let's see what you're really like.'*

*Of course the initiated have seen Tyrannosaurus Rex before so they know what's
coming and they applaud in happy anticipation. There are a few uninitiated in the
front row whose cheers are mocking for they seem to say: 'We're trouble makers
and going to be aggressive because we don't want to understand.' Funny thing is
those trouble makers are completely converted by the end of the evening, dancing
in the aisles to the rock 'n' roll sounds of Marc and Steve and digging, knowing what
it's all about. Their aggressions gentled, channelled into exhausting participation by
T.Rex [sic] with T.Rex.*

*Not a big chartname teenybopper group and therefore mildly surprising to see
just how popular they really are, but not surprising once Tyrannosaurus Rex are
on stage playing, with Marc Bolan sitting cross-legged, elfin-like, pounding rock
chords on his guitar and coupling them with old English lyrics sung in a long one-
word raga. And Steve Took harmonizing better than ever before, thumping those
war-like tomtoms into a sometimes frenzied and sometimes peaceful rhythm.*

Later Boltwood sums up the duo in a final paragraph: *S*trangely, although
*an automatic labelling machine would say: introvert music, T.Rex music is extro-
vert and becoming more so. Easier to be involved than stay cool. Marc's songs,
though, are not involved with very much that goes on outside himself – more a
reflection. Putting it all in his own terms. He's been involved in the pop business
long enough to have learnt to take life on his own terms, too, thus the reason for
success now, I feel.*

When *Unicorn* was released on 18 May, it was looked upon by the press as
Tyrannosaurus Rex's finest album to date. Indeed there were many reasons for
this. Marc had had much more time to put his ideas together, the royalties from
previous releases ensured that. But, he also seemed to have changed direction quite
subtly, with the Tolkien influences still there, plain to hear, but with a distinct
difference in the way the songs were delivered. Some of the naivety of the first
two albums had disappeared and in its place was a maturity and confidence in
the way the material was produced. The album reached a heady twelve in the UK
charts.

In June Marc Bolan the song writer became Bolan the poet when Lupus Music,

an independent publishers owned by his then manager, Brian Morrison, published a book of poetry titled *The Warlock of Love*. It was not really to sell in great numbers until Marc Bolan and T.Rex became more popular and saleable a couple of years later. Initially the book was only available by mail order with a retail price of 14s 6p, which included postage and packing. Today copies exchange hands for £50.00.

With *Unicorn* firmly under his belt, Marc turned his talents to the follow-up single. It was now that he really began to feel that the acoustic developments he had made with his music, and for which T.Rex were famous, were beginning to wear thin. Fortunately, improved finances were to allow him to experiment more and this included the acquisition of an electric guitar and the consequent development of a new sound for Tyrannosaurus Rex, unleashed to an unsuspecting United Kingdom on 25 July. As Steve Took remarked in *NME* in October 1972: *I got into playing guitar again, playing bass and we did an electric single 'King of the Rumbling Spires'. They took the end off it. I was playing drums, Nalob [Bolan] was playing guitar, I played bass and he played organ. We put on some percussion afterwards, and we were both singing, but there's only so much room for harmonies there.*

Aggression had replaced the softer tones of earlier offerings when 'King of the Rumbling Spires' stunned his growing legion of fans, many of whom did not much like what they heard: the single only reached a poor forty-four in the charts for just one week, before slipping away again.

Undeterred, at the end of summer 1969, Marc announced that Tyrannosaurus Rex were to tour America. This was not quite as grand as it might sound, in fact it appears that they spent most of their time at clubs in and around New York. The tour was a disaster; it was also the signal of the end for the Bolan–Took partnership. On returning to England, minus Steve Took, Marc announced to the press that the split was a mutual thing and there had been no bad scenes, but the news very nearly ruined Marc's career when booking agents stopped asking for Tyrannosaurus Rex, thinking it was all over for them. Marc rallied round as ever, but the almost throwaway laid-back approach to the break-up with Took hid the

true problems very well. June was quoted later in *Marc Bolan: A Tribute* as saying this of the first American tour and resultant parting of the ways: *Steve Took was very heavily into acid, but very heavily; not just an indulger, he was taking two or three trips a day. He became just like a vegetable and on stage – a stage about as big as you'd get in a tiny club that seated about one hundred people – he would suddenly start taking off his clothes and beating himself with belts and things like that....*

When you've only got two people on stage, a guitar player and a bongo player, you can't have the bongo player not playing bongo as you're left with only an acoustic guitar. There was no electric guitar then.

We left Steve in America; we abandoned him. He met this chick and said he didn't think he was coming back, so we just said for him to go. We came back to England, not knowing what we were going to do.

In two different press articles some years after the split Steve Took tells his own story: *I'd split unofficially before the American tour, but I had to go through with it and when I got back I was presented with a £2000 bill.*

In no way was Tyrannosaurus Rex doing my head any good; there was no vaguely hidden meaning. Basically Tyrannosaurus Rex started off as an underground nice thing. We weren't hung up about the bread and gradually the business took over – all I could see was money. When we split I didn't see anyone; I just went away and got totally ripped on acid and drinking and gambling – in no way could I relate to any of the commercial trips to do with the group.

And in *New Musical Express*: *We went to the States to promote the* Unicorn *album. I'd been boogying with the Pretty Things and this caused some disruption in management circles, which is why I've been loath to get involved with the business side of things because that's what music's all about, jamming. There's a lot of it going on, that's music ....*

Flower children, rushing around with revolutionaries – bad for the image. So I split after America – that was an experience.

. . .

While June and Marc may have returned to England shattered by the fact that Tyrannosaurus Rex was, for the moment at least, a non-entity, with hindsight it was the beginning of a new era for Marc Bolan. An advert was quickly placed in *Melody Maker* for a 'nice gentle guy to play bongos'. In actual fact, they need not have bothered placing the advertisement because the introduction of Mickey Finn, who was to succeed Took in the autumn of 1969, came about through a mutual friend.

Finn was born in Thornton Heath, Surrey in 1947. It was at nearby Rockmount Secondary School that the focus of his interests began to sharpen on rock music, art and motorbikes. The rock-music influences were the obvious artists of the fifties: Elvis Presley, Buddy Holly and Little Richard. Mickey saw his first live band when still at Rockmount, and this whetted his appetite for what was by then early sixties bands: the Beatles and Rolling Stones thus became his favourite groups and a later source of inspiration. But, it was actually with his third passion, art, where Mickey thought his future lay. He attended the Croydon College of Art in the mid-1960s, where he registered on a four-year course. There his work was considered good, but not his attitude; after just eleven months he quit and moved to London, where he became involved in psychedelia and the flower-power movement.

It was the time of the Beatles's *Sgt Pepper* album and Mickey's circle of friends included fashion models, painters and photographers. He was in one band called Hapsash and the Coloured Coat which folded soon after he joined. He then pursued a variety of artistic interests, but it was while painting internal murals that a friend mentioned his name to Marc.

Mickey Finn was dark and extremely good looking, the perfect match to the elfin Bolan. He was introduced to him as a painter, as a fellow artiste, which Marc found most appealing. It was only much later that Mickey admitted he had actually been working as a house painter/decorator. Assets, such as musicianship, might have been considered vital, but the lack of even this did not seem to matter to Marc. At that time Mickey could not sing and certainly had limited musical abilities, but he quite simply looked the business. With this in mind, Marc and Mickey went into retreat in Wales, where Finn had to learn a great deal in a fairly short space of time.

Astonishingly, and as a reflection of their joint determination, on 17 November the new Tyrannosaurus Rex duo recorded John Peel's BBC radio *Top Gear*, for transmission four days later. It was the first public appearance of Marc's new partner and, equally important, the first time the heavier, electric guitar orientated songs were heard. On the day this session was transmitted Marc also introduced Mickey to his first live audience at the Manchester Free Trade Hall at the start of a five date introduction tour.

. . .

The year 1970 started on a personal high as Marc Bolan's partnership with June Childe took on a new and welcome aspect. In a spontaneous moment early one morning, Marc's first words to June on waking were: 'Do you want to get married?' June now reflects on that day: *I was twenty-seven years old, had never been married and decided that as we had been living together for a long time that I'd say yes. We went to the Register Office, seeking advice on what to do, and were told we could either have a special licence to marry in a few days, or we could book and wait about three weeks. We married three days later.*

The spirit of confidence that had started the new year crossed over into Tyrannosaurus Rex's first release of 1970. The single 'By the Light of the Magical Moon' was an enchanting mixture of electric rock and spellbinding lyrics of enchanted gardens. It should have been Bolan's first major hit, but the opposite proved to be the case. The press did not seem to care for it and there were the first rumblings of 'sell out' and 'too much electric'. The fans, so faithful to the band at gigs, also turned their back on the single. Bolan, it was suggested, should return to his folk roots.

Bolan's initial reaction was one of dismay. He declared that he was giving up on singles in the UK and thereon would make only albums. The first of these, *Beard of Stars*, was released by Regal Zonophone on 22 March. It was to be the last album released under the banner of Tyrannosaurus Rex and once again proved to be too much for press and fans alike. Nevertheless, everyone was left in no doubt as to where Marc was heading musically from now on. The album contained a

mixture of whimsical, gentle tracks with more than a hint of romance: 'Prelude', 'Organ Blues' and 'Lofty Skies' were all enchanting. The real shock came, however, in form of 'Fish Heart Mighty Dawn Dart', 'Dragon's Ear' and the quite stunning 'Elemental Child', the last track being featured at live gigs to educate the audience in the new mood of Bolan. These new songs highlighted just how far Marc Bolan had progressed in his ability as a serious guitarist, yet press resistance to his capabilities was a problem that was constantly to haunt him. In an era that had spawned the likes of Eric Clapton and Jimi Hendrix, Marc sometimes found it difficult to be taken seriously by the music press; ironically, the more successful he became the harder he found it.

Beard of Stars did reasonably well, finally resting at a credible number twenty-one in the UK album charts. Bolan now felt he was on the right track and confidently spent the next five months writing and recording tracks for yet another new album.

It was now May 1970 and Marc and Mickey left for America, Marc this time more confident that he could get his music across to audiences in the States. Sadly, it was not to be. America historically had always been a year behind in the material on release from the UK and while Britain had been introduced to the new sounds of electric guitars, the US had only recently seen the release of the acoustically oriented *Unicorn* album. No wonder they were so unreceptive and found the concerts confusing. The gigs Tyrannosaurus Rex played in the US were once again small affairs, very much like those performed the previous year with Steve Took. But, it seemed that Marc's other major problem was simply that the Americans could not understand his style – acoustic or electric – at all; he eluded them and returned to England bruised, but fortunately not beaten.

·   ·   ·

Back in London, one summer evening Marc recorded a demo of a song that was originally meant to be included on the new album. The following morning he played it back and decided to go to the studio that same day so that Tony Visconti could hear it. 'Ride a White Swan' was the first Bolan-penned number to benefit from strings and once more it was Tony Visconti's talents that put the icing on the

cake. The string arrangements were to become a hallmark of the Visconti-produced sounds that were to evolve over the next few years.

At this point, there was also another, more significant change. During recording sessions Visconti had to write the titles of tracks and the names of artistes on the master tape boxes; after a while he tired of laboriously writing out in full the name Tyrannosaurus Rex and, at the end of a session one day, he abbreviated the name to T.Rex. On seeing this, Marc was furious and insisted that the name be written out in full; for the moment, Tony let it drop and left it there for some time until one day Tony wrote T.Rex and Marc made no comment. When advance copies arrived of the single 'Ride a White Swan' the label simply stated T.Rex.

'Ride a White Swan' was Marc's first Top Twenty hit single. It was also the first of their singles to be released with two tracks on the flip side, as well as featuring the only non-Bolan composition to date, Eddie Cochran's 'Summertime Blues'. It also coincided with the relaunch of Regal Zonophone as FLY. Hearsay has it that on the strength of a single Radio One play, 2000 copies were sold in London record stores. Fact or fiction, what is indisputable is that suddenly Marc Bolan was a sensation and the first tour as T.Rex, which began on 3 October 1970, the day after the single was released, became a sell out. This state of affairs was certainly helped by what was either a genuine concern for the fans, or one of the shrewdest business moves ever made: tickets to the gigs were pegged at the pre-decimal price of just 10s (50p), which assured Marc Bolan of a much younger audience, to the considerable bemusement of the older, more serious fans up till then only associated with him. Young girls started to appear at the gigs and the screaming began; many of the established Bolan followers found the change too much to handle. To them, Marc had truly sold out; he was now a pop star and while many of them could not begrudge him a hit after so many years, they certainly found the concerts no longer to their taste.

The new-found success also brought fresh problems for Marc, especially concerning the sound at gigs. In the studios this was simple as he could overdub, while Tony Visconti played bass guitar and the string sections created the big sound. On tour was another matter. Although Marc had tried to avoid expanding the band's line-up, there was no escape from the fact that kids arrived at gigs

expecting to hear what they had just left at home on their record players. They were not doing so and the expectation gap was too yawning for Marc to avoid any longer. He realized that the answer lay only in the recruitment of additional players and he acted quickly to audition and increase the band's size and capabilities.

First to arrive was Steve Currie the bass guitarist, who joined T.Rex midway through the British autumn tour. Born in Grimsby in 1947 there was only one love in Steve's life: music, and more importantly, the bass guitar. He played in the evenings around Grimsby with a band called the Rumbles, appearing every weekend at a jazz club in the city. Currie's family had hoped that he would take up medicine, but he failed to get into medical school, not being able to pass his English exams. He did, however, become a member of the Chartered Institute of Ship Brokers, but decided instead on a career in rock.

Currie moved to London in the late 1960s with the rest of his band to seek the proverbial fame and fortune, but they all found life hard in the capital and increasing debts left little choice but to return home. Steve, however, had come south with his girlfriend, who had a steady daytime job and was willing to support him financially. He decided to stay in London to give things a chance to improve. It was a wise move. While flipping casually through the pages of a music paper he saw an advertisement for a bass guitarist, which led him to Marc Bolan. He says this in *Marc Bolan: A Tribute: It was a very strange meeting because I'd always been a rocker; I'd come from an eleven-piece jazz-rock band so I thought, Jesus Christ, jingle-jangle type! But that was the point where he decided to change his career from being a mediocre star who loved flowers, to carving out a rock 'n' roll career for himself.*

On 11 December 1970, during the same week that 'Ride a White Swan' hit the number six spot in the UK singles charts, Marc's new label, FLY, released the first T.Rex album, simply entitled *T.Rex*. As much of an introduction to the new band profile as anything else, the album was like nothing recorded by them before. There was an excitement and vitality to the range of songs that was apparent from the moment the album was played. The year 1970 had ended on a high, but the best was to follow in 1971, the first of the legendary years.

3 · The Year of the Electric Warrior

'**R**ide a White Swan' was at ten in the singles charts by 2 January 1971, while *T.Rex* darted in and out of the album charts and sat disappointingly at its highest position of thirteen. By now, Marc's record company were starting to ask for a follow-up single, which Marc felt to be somewhat premature. After all, 'Ride a White Swan' still had life in it, having peaked at number two on 23 January, and he was still tentative about going down the singles road again. Follow-ups, especially, had a nasty habit of kicking him in the teeth. This basic uncertainty, however, was very unlike the newly confident Marc Bolan and fortunately for everyone proved a temporary insecurity that he soon overcame.

The final piece to the band jigsaw and that extra uncertainty was also more easily solved than had been expected. Tony Visconti had been working with a band called Legend and realized that the answer to Marc's need for a drummer lay in Bill Fyfield. This was more accidental than planned as, by Tony's own admission, Fyfield was the only drummer he was working with at that time. Tony asked Bill whether he fancied meeting up with Marc Bolan and Bill, being the relaxed easy-going kind of person he is, went along to a rehearsal with no preconceived ideas in mind.

Fyfield was born in Barking, Essex, in 1946. A former Sunday School teacher, he was originally a member of the Epics, supposedly one of the musical near successes of the late fifties. When the band split, Bill decided to form one of his own called Legend, which, as fate would have it, was produced in the studio by Tony Visconti.

At the end of the 'Hot Love' recording session Marc was impressed enough with Bill to offer him a full-time place in the band, but the name Fyfield was not considered glamorous enough as a stage name. Marc, therefore, suggested that Bill should retain the link with his old band and thus Bill Fyfield became Bill Legend. With his arrival, the first and by far the most successful T.Rex line-up was complete. It would continue for the next three years.

'Hot Love' was released on 19 February to rave reviews. Whereas 'Ride a White Swan' was an up-tempo but basic-sounding track, using only electric guitar and bass, 'Hot Love' was a laid-back, dreamy affair, with a full rhythm section,

strings and backing vocals. The addition of Steve Currie and Bill Legend had worked extremely well, a success also due to the excellent backing vocals of Howard Kaylan and Mark Volman, both originally members of the highly successful American West Coast band, the Turtles. During the period 1967–8, the band had had three hit singles in Britain with 'She'd Rather Be With Me', 'Eleanore' and their biggest hit 'Happy Together'. More recently they had been working with Frank Zappa's band, the Mothers of Invention.

In the *New Musical Express*, a review headline ran: 'T.Rex's "Hot Love" very commercial', and the review almost consumed itself with overexcitement.

Although still doing well with 'Ride a White Swan', T.Rex has elected to rush out this new disc today. Funny how the duo enjoyed only a minority appeal until the advent of its last single – and then all hell broke loose! Presumably because 'Swan' was the most commercial item the boys had then recorded. Well, if anything, this is even more commercial! It's even got a repetitive la-la chorus, in which Rex is joined by enthusiastic studio guests, and with which I'm sure you will feel compelled to sing along. The very simplicity of the number is the key to its assured popularity – plus the contagious bounce beat that's emphasized throughout by handclaps. Incidentally, this five-minute item is only one of three tracks on this maxi single, all penned by Marc Bolan. So if you buy this set, you can be confident that it's money well spent.

With the inclusion of two tracks on the flip side, 'Woodland Rock' and 'The King of the Mountain Cometh', the set, as the reviewer refers to it, had a musical running time of just over twelve minutes, a great deal for fans at a time when the average length of a single was six or seven minutes.

Within two weeks 'Hot Love' was at seventeen in the UK singles chart and just two weeks later hit the number one spot. It was Marc's first taste of life at the top and at the top is where T.Rex and the single remained for an impressive six weeks.

. . .

Early January had signalled the start of another gruelling list of tour dates that

was to stretch, with a few strategically placed breaks, through to March. T.Rex completed the first leg of their British tour at Nottingham University on 20 February, the day after the release of 'Hot Love'. It was then that Marc Bolan and his associates knew that the scene had changed; Marc, seemingly overnight, had become a rock 'n' roll star.

The first week of March was spent on a whirlwind tour of Ireland, appearing in Cork, Belfast and Dublin on consecutive days. Then, back on the mainland, T.Rex did what proved to be the last of the university-style gigs to packed houses. The problems with security had become insurmountable due to the increase in the band's popularity and Bolan, in particular, felt very personally at risk. Amazingly it was during this month that FLY, Marc's new record company, took a backward step in the promotion of T.Rex by planning the release of a *Best of* ... compilation. The album itself was part of a series of back catalogue releases by FLY (which included such acts as the Move and Procol Harum) and was advertised as containing two previously unreleased tracks 'Blessed Wild Apple Girl' and the enchanting 'Once Upon the Seas of Abyssinia'. This was all very well for the new, young fans who were buying anything that said T.Rex and it was of them that the marketing people at FLY were taking advantage. The album was entitled *The Best of T.Rex* and all fourteen tracks were Tyrannosaurus Rex recordings. Yet, the question must be raised about whether this was simply a blatant cashing in on T.Rex's new-found commercial success or a positive attempt to promote the band to their best advantage. At the time, many fans felt it was crass commercialism and sadly it was by no means the only occasion on which this was to happen in Marc's career, but this was the first and only time the band's name had been used in such a way.

In England 'Hot Love' spent the whole of April 1971 holding the number one position, while T.Rex were in America touring. It was quite frustrating for Marc to play to audiences who were still not truly switched on to the T.Rex sound. None of this was helped by the fact that at home Marc was now a superstar in the making, whereas in the States his star had barely risen. But, something good came out of the visit: it was here that Marc Bolan and T.Rex recorded their next single and put together most of the tracks for a new album planned for release that autumn.

On Marc's return to England he discovered just how popular T.Rex had become there. He also realized that the university-style gigs now had to become a thing of the past as the demand to see the new pop phenomenon of T.Rex had escalated to the point at which only major city halls could accommodate the huge number of fans. Marc again insisted that ticket prices on the new tour, which began on 9 May at the Bournemouth Winter Gardens, should be pegged at 60p. However, it was neither the price of a ticket, nor the fact that the new tour started there that put Bournemouth on the map; it was the fans.

During the day of the first gig in Bournemouth scenes there were more reminiscent of a football crowd making their way to a ground than a concert audience. Groups of teenagers milled around everywhere, wearing scarves around their necks and wrists in yellows, blues and whites, all bearing the same circular photos of Marc and the words MARC BOLAN on one side and T.REX on the other. Inside the hall, there was a very strange, almost intimidating atmosphere, an electrical tension that certainly had not featured so prominently before. Even Marc, in his heart of hearts could not possibly have been ready for the effect he had on the audience when he and the band first stepped on stage. Girls simply jumped from their seats and dashed towards them to build up a solid wall of screaming teenagers, who began to claw themselves closer to the new messiah of rock, so single minded in their efforts that they tore off each other's clothes and ripped at flesh. Nothing mattered but to get as close as they could. Fans at the back of the hall stood no chance of seeing the band and they simply looked at each other and resigned themselves to taking a back seat to events unfolding before them. The scenes were to be repeated throughout the thirteen dates of the three-week tour.

On 25 June the news was announced in the music press that a new T.Rex single was to be rush released on Friday of the following week. 'Get It On' was the single that had been recorded in Los Angeles during the most recent tour of America. Backing vocals were supplied once again by Kaylan and Volman, with the addition of Ian McDonald, formerly saxophonist with King Crimson. The announcement also told of two new live dates, the last to be held before the next full tour in the autumn, at the Birmingham Odeon on 2 July and London's Lewisham Odeon on 9 July.

· · ·

THE YEAR OF THE ELECTRIC WARRIOR

If the first six months of 1971 were chaotic, what was to follow can only be described as nothing short of manic. 'Get It On' took just two weeks to hit the top spot in the singles charts and give Marc his second number one in the space of four months. Technically it contained not two but three flip-side tracks with 'Raw Ramp', 'There Was a Time' and 'Electric Boogie'. But their new-found success did not come without its disadvantages and there were now danger signs for the personal safety of Marc and the rest of the band. The more successful they became, the more security was needed. It got to a stage where just getting the short distance from the stage door to the cars meant taking their lives in their hands. Once outside, girls would simply launch themselves at the cars, climbing on to the roofs. The most unnerving episodes occurred when they hammered on the windows and could be heard scratching away on the roof, trying desperately to get at Marc and Mickey. It was fan mania not seen since the sixties and the prime of the Beatles and the Rolling Stones.

Rock journalist Steve Peacock has written vividly about the Lewisham gig of 9 July and clearly illustrates the problem: *O*utside the dressing-room window a crowd of girls were chanting: 'We want Marc, we want Marc, Marc, Marc, Mickee!' They'd been doing it all evening, inside the theatre during the interval, screaming all through the first T.Rex set of the evening, and now outside the window between houses. They got Marc – at least Marc stuck his head out of the window: 'Screeeeeam!' Marc came back across the room and sat down....

The mood in the dressing room was subdued as Marc had just heard that Jim Morrison's death had been confirmed. 'Everyone laughed when I said there is no time,' he said, 'but now I know that it's right – I've got to give everything now, while I can. Hendrix wasted the last two years of his life; just think what he could have done in that time. There is no time, I may not be here in two years, I don't know.'

It was time to go on stage for the final set. The band waited in the wings while Marc opened the set with an amazing solo electric guitar number, using pedals and feedback and a remarkable sense of time and dynamics. Without wishing in any way to belittle Marc's work, I got strong memory flashes of Hendrix as he stood

alone on that stage, playing that guitar as if it was as much a part of his body as an arm or a leg. The band joined him for 'One Inch Rock', then Marc did a solo song called 'Girl' with Spanish guitar, sitting cross-legged on the floor in a blue spotlight. Then there was 'Deborah' with Mickey Finn on hand drums, then back to the full band for 'Ride a White Swan', 'Hot Love' and 'Get It On'.

The house erupted, and they came back for a stomping encore of 'Summertime Blues'. There are very few rock musicians around who have that understanding of an audience combined with a feel and understanding of rock music that allows them to reach such a wide audience. The screaming ladies love it, everyone backstage loved it, and quite honestly I can't imagine anyone who could remain unmoved by it if they have any feeling at all for rock music. Marc Bolan is giving us all he has, and while I wouldn't want rock to be solely T.Rex, I wouldn't like to be without them.

There was yet more press attention to come when on 24 July in the Record Mirror, *rock journalist Val Mabbs interviewed a very confident and totally relaxed Marc Bolan:* 'Sometimes we get a very very young audience, but otherwise we get heads,' Marc told me. 'We sometimes get the screamers, anywhere but London. It always happens for us. In fact in Newcastle they broke down the front of the hall, and in Glasgow we had to get the police to get us out! But if the kids are sensible I don't dislike it. They only usually scream at the end of numbers or if you put a lot of energy into a number. The more one gyrates about the more you're going to get the kids grooving, but before we were never a visual band, ever. ELP [Emerson, Lake and Palmer] got themselves banned from a lot of places because you can throw the crowd into total hysteria, and now there is nowhere left for them to play. One does have to be careful, or the crowd might tear the building down!'*

Marc, like the Rolling Stones, the Who and many others, admits to being a rock-based pop singer, though he doesn't see himself as a pop star. He also realizes that many of the audience come to watch him on stage, but fondly hopes that they think about the music when they leave the hall for home. T.Rex's next album Electric Warrior *is currently being mixed by Marc for probable release in August.*

Though the title might convey an all electric progressive album, in fact several of the numbers are gentle acoustic songs.

'I just liked the title,' grinned Marc. 'It's one of the numbers on the album. Seven out of the ten tracks were recorded in America in Los Angeles and New York, mainly because Mark Volman and Howard Kaylan, the two Mothers [of Invention] who worked on the album, were there. I'd like to use them all the time if I could. There was also a certain element of time. Everybody else says this album is different for us, but to me it's not. I find it easier now to get the sound here that we've been getting in America, if you see what I mean. It's very easy to get. They use cheap microphones and they don't have any screens at all in the studio.'

But didn't Marc think that might be a step backwards in achieving the clear-cut sound now possible? 'I never wanted that!' He explained and a slow smile emerged. After achieving what he terms as 'our first biggie' with three million sales of 'Hot Love', Marc has obviously no need to worry!

August gave Marc and the band a well-deserved break. There was actually only one gig during that month when T.Rex appeared at the Weeley Festival, one of the those three-day-event specialities that had started during the sixties. On a hot August Bank Holiday weekend, the acts that appeared alongside Marc Bolan and T.Rex included Barclay James Harvest, King Crimson, the Faces and Lindisfarne.

September could also have been classed as slow, except for the fact that on the 17th the most important Marc Bolan album to date was issued. *Electric Warrior* was by far the most impressive album ever recorded by Marc. All the ingredients were there: romance, blues, mythology and good old rock 'n' roll. This was combined with breathtaking arrangements and production by the master himself, Tony Visconti. There was another special ingredient: fun. It was clearly audible by listening to the album that a great time had been had by all in making it, performed as it also was with supreme confidence. *Electric Warrior* was the last album under Marc's existing recording contract with FLY and the band's first number one album. If Marc had been able to blueprint his career, he could not have planned it better. He was in demand, red hot. As far as his musical career and recording future were concerned he could name his own price.

Electric Warrior was met by rave reviews and amongst them one powerful written analysis of both the album and its influences appeared in *Sounds*, one of the leading music papers of the day, written by Nick Logan. *B*olan's roots are *far reaching, and thoroughly researched. Both 'Hot Love', with its echoes of 'At the Hop' – unintentional as they may have been – and the current 'Get It On', shades of Chuck Berry and the rawness of recording that invokes memories of the old Sun Studios, evidently draw their source of power from the very back of the rock 'n' rolling Bolan's head.... Bolan has so cunningly utilized a panorama of influences – as wide-ranging as his record collection, stretching through early Presley to his score or so of official and unofficial Hendrix albums – that anyone who has travelled a similar path will find his head spinning from one nostalgia to the next.*

On 'Monolith' you might be listening to a '71 remake of 'Duke of Earl'. 'Cosmic Dancer' has strings which could have been scored by Bert Berns. 'Jeepster' might have been cut in Sam Phillip's midget Sun Studios, and nearer home the jamming 'Lean Woman Blues' could be an unused Bob Dylan tape from 'Bringing It All Back Home'. That's taking it right down to basics of course. On top of that Bolan has added a spicy icing and a cultured producer's ear to produce a finished product very much '71 and very much his own....

Electric Warrior is certainly a major achievement in Bolan's career, both as performer and producer. Seven of the eleven tracks are American recordings, cut either in New York or at Wally Heider's San Francisco studios, the rest, recordings made in London. Marc hasn't lost any of the basic rawness of the American tracks by the addition at various points of Tony Visconti's string arrangements and contributions from other musicians like Ian McDonald's saxes and Rick Wakeman's organ.

'I am very aware', says Marc, 'that for the kids who bought the singles this is the first album. And if you bought a single I don't see how you could be disappointed with it. On the other hand I don't personally see how anyone who has a head at all, who liked us in the past, could not like it.'

In October 1971 T.Rex began their *Electric Warrior* tour, the second major

UK tour of the year. It was a sell-out and took in a gruelling twenty dates in little over three weeks. Starting at the Portsmouth Guildhall on 19 October then on to, Plymouth ABC on the 20th, Cardiff Capitol on the 21st and Sheffield City Hall on the 23rd. At Croydon Fairfield Hall (24th), a second house was played as a result of the original gig selling out in fifty minutes. Bradford St George's Hall (25th) was the next stop, followed by Brighton Dome (27th), Glasgow Green's Playhouse (29th), and Newcastle City Hall (31st). In November the gigs were Stockton ABC (4th), Birmingham Town Hall (5th), Manchester Free Trade Hall (6th), Leicester's De Montfort Hall (8th), Lincoln ABC (9th), and Wigan ABC on the 10th should have been the final venue. However, such had been the demand that T.Rex swiftly moved on to the Liverpool Stadium for two shows on 11 November.

Although this proved a hectic time for Bolan, he had not only the tour to occupy his thoughts. With his recording contract with FLY about to come to an end, he had acquired the business advisory services of Tony Secunda to help him to negotiate a new deal. Secunda had been involved with a string of successful acts, either in an advisory role or managing them himself: Johnny Kidd and the Pirates, the Moody Blues, Procol Harum, and the Move. He introduced Mick Taylor to the Rolling Stones after Brian Jones left and had managed Alan White once with the Plastic Ono Band and Yes. After Cream split up he was a major contributor to the formation of Blind Faith and also represented Denny Laine, originally with the Moody Blues, who then went on to join Paul and Linda McCartney's Wings. At long last, with Secunda's help, Bolan felt secure that his interests were being well served.

The possibility of changing from being just another artist on someone else's record label actually to controlling his own was a fairly well-kept secret. When the news did break, it was *Melody Maker* that disclosed Marc Bolan's plan to form his own record label, following in the footsteps of the Beatles, the Rolling Stones and the Moody Blues. EMI, however, were keen to see Marc remain on one of their labels – Regal Zonophone and FLY were both distributed by EMI – and therefore were putting together a package that would, they felt, keep Marc 'extremely happy'.

Marc himself said to *Melody Maker*: *The label situation is that we haven't done a deal yet. We are having a meeting at the moment to suss that very question. It is very possible that I may have my own label. I want to do that and I want the best quality product at the best prices. I would like to record other artistes very much too.*

It would be pure speculation to ask whether Marc would have stayed with the FLY label, but what was well known is Marc's displeasure at the release of the 'new' single. This may well have twisted his arm away from them, making him more keen than ever to structure the development of his career, with the fate of his recordings being held firmly in his own hands. 'Jeepster' was released on 1 November and by the last week of that same month it occupied the number two position in the UK singles chart behind the band that, at the time, were Marc's closest rivals: Slade with 'Coz I Luv You'. With the exception of the first week's chart of December when 'Jeepster' slipped to number three, T.Rex spent the remainder of 1971 at number two. Which rock artist kept Marc from his third successive number one? Was it Tom Jones? Was it the Carpenters? Was it Cliff Richard? No, it was actually comedian Benny Hill with a little ditty called 'Ernie, the Fastest Milkman in the West'!

The life of 'Jeepster' – taken from the *Electric Warrior* album and backed with another track from the album *Life's a Gas* – as a single actually began as a limited edition, special preview 7-inch disc. It was meant simply to be a special thank you by T.Rex to everyone in the business who had supported them throughout 1971. Evidence tends to support Bolan's assertion that he knew nothing about its general release by FLY, if for no other reason than that it was the first T.Rex single to be issued with only one flip-side title.

Yet, without a shadow of a doubt 1971 had seen the birth of an Electric Warrior in the shape of Marc Bolan. T.Rex had two best-selling singles in the 1971 Top Ten listings, the only act to do so that year. *Electric Warrior* was ranked the fifth best-selling album of 1971 and, not surprisingly, T.Rex were voted, by a music-press poll, best band of 1971.

4 · T.Rextasy

The new year 1972 started with a joyous and resounding bang for Marc Bolan, with months of speculation over the recording contract and label deal finally ending on Monday, 3 January, when he announced the formation of his own record label The T.Rex Wax Co. For their part, EMI were also delighted with the arrangement as T.Rex were to continue to be distributed by them. What was obviously most important to Marc now was that he controlled his own destiny; he and he alone would decide what singles were to be released and when.

That the initial offering of 1972 – the first single on the new T.Rex Wax Co label – would be a hit was a safe bet, but even EMI were reportedly staggered when advance orders ensured a release-day figure in excess of 90,000 copies. The following week, as 'Jeepster' disappeared from the singles chart, 'Telegram Sam', backed with 'Cadillac' and 'Baby Strange', entered at number three, the highest ever first-week placing.

T.Rex did only one gig in England during January – at the Boston Starlight Club in Lincolnshire on the 15th which went down well with the fans. Admission price was held at 60p. It was considered very much a warm-up for the first major European tour that was to take them away from England at the end of the month.

On the chart published for week commencing 2 February, T.Rex had done it again. The coveted number one position was theirs for the third time in four attempts. Not that they were in England to celebrate; this they had to do from America where they were touring for most of the month. But the celebrations would not have lasted long, in any case, as the top spot in the UK charts was theirs for a mere two weeks before 'Son of My Father' by Chicory Tip knocked them into second place where they stayed for the remainder of the month.

It was during this time that rumours started to fly about whether Marc Bolan was to retire altogether from touring. 'Not true' was the reaction from the T.Rex camp; after all the band were now touring America. But, nevertheless, the rumours had some grounding in truth, the point being that Marc was simply finding it increasingly difficult to handle the reactions of his English fans; the horrendous problems of security, it appeared were his chief concern.

Although America did not generate fears for his personal safety, it had its own

problem areas for T.Rex and was proving nowhere near as easy to crack as England. While Marc was chalking up a third number one in England the Americans were, on the whole, disinterested. The eight-venue tour of the States had kicked off in Seattle on 11 February and was followed by dates in Los Angeles, Philadelphia, Boston, Washington, Chicago, Detroit, Cleveland and ending finally at the Carnegie Hall, New York, on 27 February.

Back in the United Kingdom, T.Rex had gone some way to appease both fans and press alike when it was announced that they would be appearing at the Empire Pool Wembley Arena in London on Saturday, 18 March. For the moment, it seemed, Marc's fears about security were being handled. The ticket price was 75p and the gig sold out within days, which was hardly surprising considering all the uncertainty around whether T.Rex would tour again; it was, after all, the only UK date to be announced in the press that year.

As it turned out, the concert was an extra special occasion with the afternoon and evening performances filmed by Ringo Starr, ex-Beatle drummer turned film-maker/director, for a documentary to be released by Apple Films sometime in the future. Film or no film, it was a magical day and for the 20,000 fans who were lucky enough to be there, either during the afternoon matinée performance or for the evening show, its memory will live on for ever. Amid the screaming headlines in the music press the following weekend, BOLAN'S TRIUMPH and TWENTY THOUSAND SCREAMERS AND THE DAY THAT POP CAME BACK were just two of the headlines that delighted Marc and his fans alike. There was another leading header, though, that summed it all up: MONSTER POWER!

The Empire Pool, a massive complex, played host to T.Rex on that glorious day, unaware that what it was about to witness was nothing short of total adulation. The scenes outside were similar to those normally associated with gatherings in another part of Wembley for the Football Association's Cup Finals and Inter-nationals. The only difference between the two crowds being that down at the road at Wembley Stadium there were two sides to shout for, whereas at the Empire Pool everyone was on the same side, coming together to pay homage to one man, Marc Bolan. Touts outside the complex were asking £4.00 and £5.00 for a 75p ticket. Unofficial programmes, posters and scarves were on sale everywhere and eager fans

paid over the odds for anything, wanting to grasp everything on offer, not aware, at that point, that official merchandise was on sale inside the domain of T.Rex's lair.

All around groups of people were gabbling excitedly, a sea of children's faces witnessing one thousand Christmases all rolled into one. Ushered like cattle through doorways into the main hall, the first impressions were of a vast tiered galaxy of seats, rows upon rows of them. Looking skywards, other constellations of fans seemed to move around the heavens as the lights from the roof of the complex twinkled like small isolated stars. The gangway stretched ahead like the winding road to the castle in the *Wizard of Oz*, except the wizard here was easier to find. In the distance at the front of the auditorium was an apparently tiny stage: was the whole band really going to fit on that? Moving forwards to find a seat, the backdrop images of Marc became clearer, as did a huge cardboard cut-out of him on the right of the arena. As fans walked tentatively towards their seats, suddenly there was nothing to see but an ocean of Bolan lookalikes. The audience bobbed up and down in their seats like swimmers in a strong sea. They were nervous with excitement, trying to decide whether to sit down or stand up for a better view.

Quiver came on stage first as the support band, an appropriate name for anyone who had to play first to an audience that really were not at all interested in them. This turned out to be an especially unfair assessment of their talents as they performed well. As their set finished and the applause died away, there was a new tension of expectation: the wizard himself would soon grace the arena with his presence. Emperor Rosko, a popular DJ of the early 1970s, was doing his best to keep the crowd entertained by playing records, when suddenly the whole atmosphere changed and the chanting of Marc's name got louder and louder.

'It's star time ... they're just back from a coast-to-coast tour of America ... it's —' and the rest of the Emperor's introduction was wiped out in a blast of cheering, screaming voices. Bill Legend and Steve Currie were first in view, followed shortly by Mickey Finn, who waved as screams greeted him; and then, in that split second of time when the audience shivers from the emotion of it all, Marc, the main man, appeared on stage and all hell broke loose. By this time the fans acted like slaves to their emotional reactions as they resigned themselves to the pressure

and pleasure of the experience and the entire audience welded itself together, with each fan feeling themselves somehow glued in the middle.

Over an hour of music followed, which was hard to appreciate with so many other things to think about. The fans must have wondered if they would survive the experience at all as they withstood the breathless crush of the crowd and felt the urge to panic. But Bolan's performance proved mesmerizing and a distraction from such fears as they followed Bolan's every move. At one point miniature tambourines were thrown into the audience, causing another surge forwards as those at the back realized that Bolan was not an athlete and able to throw the tiny musical replicas to reach them far back in the crowd. Only those nearer the front stood a chance of catching one. Yet, suddenly a young man caught one of these gifts from God in his hands, only to succumb to the pleading glances of a beautiful glitter-dusted girl to hand it over to her. The fan rejoined the pack and then could not believe his luck when another tambourine, launched from his idol's own hand in apparent slow motion, landed in his outstretched palm. 'Thanks Marc,' he silently mouthed, believing that Bolan had personally witnessed his earlier compassion. To his left, another face looked pained and hopeful, but getting the first was lucky, the second direct from Marc, and this time he hung on to his prize, not pushing his luck for a third gamble.

Suddenly it was all over; Marc waved and disappeared from sight. But the fans would not believe it and the chanting started up again, telling the band not to leave without one more glimpse, please. After what appeared an eternity for the fans, poised on the brink of a wave of expectation, T.Rex came back on stage to launch into 'Summertime Blues', the Cochran rock 'n' roll classic. Then it really was all over and slowly the huge audience left the complex, only then to realize the uniqueness of the occasion as something to savour for ever.

Marc was interviewed later by Steve Peacock for *Sounds* and during the interview was asked how it felt to be on stage, for example at Wembley, and be aware that a vast auditorium of people were focused on him, idolizing him at the same time? *I'm more concerned about whether my guitar's in tune, to be honest. There's too much to think about on stage because I know that if I stop playing, or*

if no one plays for ten minutes, the whole thing will be a shambles. So you try to keep the motion of the show together.

Marc was then asked whether he realized just how seriously the kids took him; to Marc it may be just a 'jive', to the kids, though, it's much more.

He responds with: *It's nothing to do with me. I'm what I am and I can't change what I am. I do what I do, and I respond – it's all the same thing, it's one. Without them, I'm just a poet. With them I'm a rock and roll star – trophies man, like rhinoceros heads. I didn't shoot them though. I didn't shoot the rhinoceros. That's the difference.*

The same week in which all the papers were full of heady reviews of the Empire Pool gig, FLY, T.Rex's recently discarded record company started to reissue a batch of old releases. This was something that was to anger Bolan as well as return to haunt him over time. The initial reissue was the very first Tyrannosaurus Rex single 'Debora', released as part of a maxi single containing three other Tyrannosaurus Rex titles, 'One Inch Rock', 'Woodland Bop' and 'The Seal of Seasons'. It eventually peaked at number seven in the singles charts. With Marc being very much against its release, on the surface this would appear contradictory because, as FLY rightly commented, he was earning royalties. There was, however, a real conflict of interest within Marc himself and although FLY were unsympathetic to his displeasure, choosing to see only his financial gain, his problem really centred on the musical development of the band. It is highly likely that Marc was struggling with the fact that the reissues were ancient history and did not represent musically where he now wanted T.Rex to be seen. When asked for his reaction to the release, he was quoted in *Melody Maker* on 29 April as saying: *I'd like to make the point that it's nothing to do with me. They're obviously going to keep putting those records out, so I've been told. Of course they are. They've got a lot of product. They've got five other ones that we probably know the titles of, which would be potentially biggies now.*

But FLY say it's impossible to release them without your permission? Marc continues: *I know. Legally, that's what they told me. Legally that's true. Mean-*

while, I think 'Debora' is at number five now. In five records time I'd probably injunct them. But I just don't wanna do all that. That's the last thing the kids need. We'll squash them with the new one in five minutes. I just wish I had it ready sooner so I could put it out the second week and squash them altogether.

Marc Bolan received an open letter from FLY records, following his remarks in the music press about his displeasure at the reissue, signed by label manager David Ruffell. *Your comments in last week's press struck us as being a little odd, to say the least, and we would like the chance to clear up several points.*

The record was issued, not on the regular FLY label, but as one of a series of, initially four, Magni Flys intended to make available again classic recordings in maxi-single form. It was never promoted as the follow-up to 'Telegram Sam' and we even took the trouble to put the series out in a special sleeve with photographs taken from around the time of the original release. Even the label says Tyrannosaurus Rex and not T.Rex.

You also say that 'Debora' is unrepresentative of what you are doing at the moment, but when we saw you not so long ago you were still performing it acoustically and better than ever. Own up, Marc, 'Debora' was great then and always will be. If your fans want to buy it on a single with three other tracks, then surely that's their right. Keep boppin'!!

The reissue of 'Debora' had obviously upset Marc Bolan a great deal, yet what is most strange is that when FLY released the first two Tyrannosaurus Rex albums as a double pack, not a word was heard from him. Within four weeks it held the number one slot in the album charts.

During April, while the Tyrannosaurus Rex reissues were soaring up the album charts, London Weekend Television screened one of their series of *Music in the Round*, previously recorded on 8 December 1971. T.Rex performed live without the aid of backing tracks to a selected studio audience. They blasted through 'Telegram Sam', 'Cadillac', 'Jeepster' and an amazing version of 'Spaceball Ricochet'. It was an all too rare occurrence, but one well worth the effort. Marc was at his most relaxed when he was interviewed by Humphrey Burton between songs and handled the occasion well. It was clear that Burton had no idea how to

deal with Bolan, and obviously did not understand what all the fuss was about.

Humphrey Burton kicked off the interview after T.Rex had opened the set with 'Jeepster': 'Is "Jeepster", by any stretch of the imagination rock – or is it something different?' Marc responded:

'It's '70's rock – as opposed to the earlier stuff. The earlier stuff was great, but the recordings were basic.'

Burton then went on to ask Marc about the song 'Cadillac': 'I noticed that a lot of your songs are about cars – are cars important?'

'Yes,' replied Marc who then goes on to expand, 'I've got an American Cadillac, given to me by a friend, it's a work of art – I don't drive but it's an incredible piece of art.'

'A lot of people', Burton then comments, 'have criticized your kind of music – my generation and beyond – for being too loud. You don't think that – obviously?'

Marc explains, 'It's kind of an expression – it's an art form where you use volume to express yourself. Volume allows you to get more into the music.'

'Yes, but,' continues Burton, 'many people are saying the music is monotonous and that it is only loud.'

Marc's face clouds over, obviously a little put out.

'A lot of people say a lot of things about a lot of stuff. You know many of them are not well informed on what they are talking about! Rock music is easily as important as any other music. Music is a thing one feels about and enjoys and if one does not feel and enjoy, then one shouldn't talk about it – or listen to it.'

Burton is obviously enjoying Marc's reaction as he continues: 'So what do you mean by more important? Do you mean a lot more people get pleasure and excitement out of this than any other kind of music?'

'Yeah,' Marc confirms, 'as a kid I hated classical music.'

The subject then moves on to the 100-watt speakers towering in the background. 'Why,' asks Burton, 'do you have these huge loudspeakers?'

Marc becomes relaxed again as he answers, 'Well, basically, most of the halls we play in are very big, consequently you would not hear us at the back.'

'How big are you audiences?' Burton asks.

'Normally around 5000,' Marc proudly replies.

Humphrey is stunned, '5000! Well we've only got about 1500 in here – so this is —'

And before he can go on Marc interrupts, saying, 'This, is a small room.'

Burton is not to be put off and gets on the loudness trail again. 'But then when you've got that enormous big sound —'

Marc interrupts again, slightly exasperated, 'Yeah, but in a hall your playing it's not always necessarily very loud.'

'Comfortable?' asks Burton.

'Yeah – comfortable,' responds Marc.

'But all the same – normally its forte rather than piano – loud rather than soft. Don't you ever long for the quietness of a unaccompanied piece?' queries Burton.

'We – well, you know, on stage we do four or five acoustic numbers.'

Burton then moves on to the lyrics of Marc's songs and begins by quoting from the acoustic number Marc had just performed, 'Spaceball Ricochet'. 'It's a real poem that rhymes – not simply like the earlier songs?'

'No, lyrically,' Marc says, 'it's probably one of the most important songs I've written.'

'Were you influenced by any poets? There are many rich words in your book *The Warlock of Love* – where did you gather them from?'

Marc looks seriously at Burton, 'I don't really know – I believe I was, in a previous life, some kind of bard. Most of the things I write about are descriptions of places I've obviously never been to and most of the words I write, you won't find in any dictionary anywhere – and', Marc owns up to with a smile, 'I spell appallingly.'

Burton then invites members of the audience to ask Marc questions. A young girl asks, 'Do you get more satisfaction out of writing poetry or singing songs?'

Marc answers, 'If I'm pleased with a poem I'm satisfied, if I'm pleased with a song I'm satisfied – there's really no difference. Many people say, "Why don't you make music like you used to?" – I think I am – I only make what I wanted to play.'

Another young girl then asks which group of people Marc thinks he appeals to most, just the young girls, or lots of different groups of people.

'There are not just young girls here,' Marc states.

Burton interjects, 'They are mostly young girls – come on, Marc, let's not get away from the fact. I'd say they were 90 per cent – I'm not saying anything against them – it's very nice!'

Marc responds, 'I hope that anyone who takes their music seriously, takes me seriously. People I work with – there is a mutual respect and artistically that's all I can ask for.'

The reviews that followed the show were scathing of Humphrey Burton and his interview of Bolan. The following is how one unidentified reviewer saw the experience. *Marc Bolan's appearance on London Weekend Television's* Music in the Round *was embarrassing through no fault of his own. The interviewer, Humphrey Burton, was obviously totally at a loss for constructive comment or discussion, his script was appalling and his discomfort blatantly apparent. Bolan did his best with the inane questions, but the flat atmosphere of the studios couldn't have helped. The audience looked as though they couldn't have cared less about the band and could have been watching the* Epilogue *for all the interest they showed in the music. The entire show looked very third rate and shoddy, the only bright spots being the actual music. And as Marc referred to 'Telegram Sam' being their possible new single, it shows how long ago it was recorded, too. Bolan deserves better.*

.   .   .

On 5 May the T.Rex Wax Co issued 'Metal Guru' and FLY released a great hits package entitled *Bolan Boogie* on the very same day. Quite coincidentally (unlike the release date) both the single and the album reached number one in their respective charts, just two weeks later on 20 May. Now, FLY could proudly boast their third number one Bolan album in a row, a feat that the T.Rex Wax Co unfortunately would never match. The *Bolan Boogie* package contained thirteen tracks, of which four tracks were the hits of 1971, plus, once again, a selection of Tyrannosaurus Rex titles.

Bolan commented to the press: *I'm not at all happy about it and the remarks I made about the reissue of 'Debora' apply equally to this album. Still, if the kids want to buy it, right on. It's flattering that people want to turn back the clock, as long as they realize it has nothing to do with what we are presenting now.*

According to Marc, 'Metal Guru' was an easy choice for a follow-up single and an easy song to record in contrast to others: 'The band laid down their basic tracks in under two hours and went home while Tony and me stayed on to get my guitar playing perfect. Which actually took a few more hours.' The engineers were then allowed to go home so that just Marc and Tony were left to give the sounds the feel they needed. Marc explained further: 'The engineers are good guys, but we like to make the subtle changes in the sound that they might miss.' With 'Metal Guru', Marc then travelled to Los Angeles to get his Mothers [of Invention] team to put down the backing vocals.

'I think,' said Bolan, 'that "Metal Guru" is my finest single yet.' The flip-side tracks 'Thunderwing' and 'Lady' are pretty classy, too. Marc went on to explain a little more about 'Lady': *The intro to 'Lady' is Lennon and McCartney's 'Eight Days a Week', intentionally. The rest of it is like a Sun oldie, a nice groove track, vaguely Spectorish with twelve acoustic guitars. It has the most instruments I've ever used, with mellotron, and Howard and Mark's back-up vocals.'*

On 6 May, Marc announced to the press that T.Rex were to go back on the road for a summer tour. This news was greeted with some surprise as originally the Wembley gigs were to have been the last British dates that year until the autumn tour. 'The reaction at Wembley was such a gas,' said Bolan. 'Many fans have complained that they could not get to London and so we are going to them, as we have done in the past.' The Birmingham Odeon on 9 June was to be followed by Cardiff Capitol on the 10th, Manchester Belle Vue on the 16th and Newcastle City Hall on the 24th. It was also confirmed that there were to be two gigs at each venue with the exception of Manchester.

If confirmation were needed that the tours were getting out of hand then the dates in June did just that. It was mayhem. Marc emerged from one gig with

bruised ribs after a fight for his life when cornered by three female fans, all brandishing scissors and intent on taking a 'souvenir' from his head. The days of inviting one or two fans backstage to take a single lock of hair were well and truly over. It was never made official that T.Rex were finished with touring in England, but the autumn tour promised just months earlier never materialized. With a certain degree of accuracy, the finger can be pointed at the fans' behaviour to explain Marc's absence from England's shores. His personal safety was quite simply being put more and more at risk. It is also clear that this was possibly the first mistake Marc made in judging the mood of his fans and it cost him dearly later in terms of his popularity. It would be two years on – with the exception of two Christmas shows – before Marc toured England again, by which time a great deal was to have changed.

．　　．　　．

On top of the difficulties Marc was having with hero worship he also had an old record company problem to sort out – and fast. Track records had discovered some old demos from Marc's pre-Tyrannosaurus Rex days under Simon Napier Bell's management, which they announced they were going to release. The album was to be called *Hard On Love*. Marc, while admitting defeat with FLY and their constant stream of reissues, ensured that Track knew exactly what he thought of their plans by taking out a high-court writ against them, demanding that they withdraw the album. This they did immediately and put all ideas on ice to comply with the strictures of the writ.

On a happier note, advance orders of 100,000 was the reception that greeted the long-awaited release of *The Slider* on 23 July. Recorded earlier in the year it was well received and during its first week reached number four in the album charts; it appeared that a fourth number one album within a twelve-month span was on the cards. Sadly it was not meant to be and *The Slider*, for all its slick sexuality, slowly dropped away over the coming weeks, to leave the question unanswered about whether the lack of 'personal' promotion had any bearing on its poor staying power. Marc himself considered the album his finest to date, 'But I always say that, don't I?' was his comment, delivered with a smile. *The Slider*

was important to Marc because it was the first album in which he had been lyrically true to himself. Many of the songs were self-portraits, some quite sad and the beautiful 'Spaceball Ricochet', in particular, has always been acknowledged as an autobiographical title. Many people have expressed surprise that it was never released as a single, but when the suggestion was put to Marc he felt it unwise to do so as he considered the number too laid back and not a suitable track for discos.

At the end of August, controversy surrounded Marc's decision not to appear in France on a four-date tour. It was apparently cancelled because of reports from the French venues that ticket sales were disappointing. Not so, retorted the Bolan camp; their version was lack of time in preparing for the forthcoming American tour and with that, T.Rex left on a flight to Montreal, Canada, for a single gig on 7 September.

This was the beginning of T.Rex's second American adventure of the year and it did not get off to a good start. The band, or more importantly Marc Bolan, could not get the audience moving much at all. Initially the atmosphere was none too friendly, with dissent from the front of the audience as first they heckled Bolan, and then stood up – not out of excitement, but pure bloody mindedness – to spoil the view of the fans seated behind them. At one point Bolan, who had been giving the set his all, stopped and shouted into the microphone,

'I feel that we're working damned hard up here, and not getting much response.' He was demanding a reaction and yet he was quoted later, with reference to the Montreal concert, as saying: 'The gig was about twenty miles from the city. Plus we had sound problems we don't usually have. I don't think we'll have to work that hard again on this tour.' And he added: 'At one point I thought I was going to die. I really did. But I don't mind lying on the floor. Whatever it takes.'

The day after the Montreal workhouse on 8 September while Marc Bolan and T.Rex were on their way to New York, 'Children of the Revolution' was released in Britain. It entered the charts at a comparatively low number fourteen – the last to have come in so low was 'Get It On' in 1971 – but the following week soared to number two sitting in behind Slade, who were enjoying their third week at number one with 'Mama Weer All Crazee Now'. Everyone got ready for a fifth number one, but it did not happen. First, David Cassidy blocked Marc and

then along came Lieutenant Pigeon with 'Mouldy Old Dough'. 'Children of the Revolution' never recovered; it spent the four weeks of October moving down the charts a few places at a time. It was, however, to become the anthem for Bolan's followers, with a driving, throbbing beat that took a hold and unleashed all the emotions of growing up.

'I've gotta Rolls-Royce 'cos it's good for my voice' and the rallying chorus sang,

'You won't fool the children of the revolution.'

These were classic lines of a classic song in an all-to-dreary, mixed-up chart – with a few notable exceptions. There, of course, is a bittersweet irony as the anthem could have carried a warning to Marc himself: fooling his own fans could be a mistake.

As 'Children' took its course in England, Marc Bolan was attempting to conquer America. Describing it later as an 'adventure tour', Bolan had acquired the fuller choral-style sound he wanted at gigs by using Aretha Franklin's backing singers on most of the dates, as well as Joe Cocker's singers when in Los Angeles. By his own admission, part of Bolan's problems in America were caused by the fact that T.Rex were not a singles band. 'Get It On' titled 'Bang a Gong' in the States – because the original title was a sexual term in the American language – was the only Top Ten hit in the US selling in excess of one million copies. The other releases did nothing.

'It's only through lack of airplay,' Bolan was to surmise, 'much like we had in the beginning in England. I'm convinced that things like "Magical Moon" and "Rumbling Spires" would have been hits if they had been played.' More likely Bolan's problem was that while he considered himself the rock 'n' roll Tolkien underground poet for American consumption, once on stage he was actually coming across as a sexual glider. In the States this made him an unknown quantity and lack of familiarity bred rejection.

In November 1972 T.Rex toured Australia and the Far East, where scenes reminiscent of the English reaction started to filter through gradually, but somehow did not have the same effect on Marc. *The Slider* was number one in Japan when the tour began in Tokyo on 28 November. The promoters there had hired a

complete clothes store for a Marc Bolan reception where they also sold Marc Bolan style clothes – such hype was typical of the well-oiled promotional machinery in Japan.

As December dawned T.Rex released their fourth single of the year when 'Solid Gold Easy Action' burst on to the scene. It finished the year at number three and would go one place higher in the first week of 1973. It was, incidentally, the first T.Rex single to have only one track on the flip side since 'By the Light of the Magical Moon' was released in 1970 and this would remain the policy until 1975.

The new single was quickly followed by the announcement of the première of the motion picture *Born to Boogie* on the 14th. This was the documentary shot earlier in the year at the Empire Pool Wembley by Ringo Starr and his team. Its reception by the media was poor, but the fans loved it, which is only natural considering Marc and T.Rex had all but starved them of live action over recent months. Furthermore, this was the age before pop-promo videos, when even two or three months of not seeing your idol could be soul destroying for fans.

Marc had very much enjoyed the filming of *Born to Boogie* and explained how it all began one day when, 'Originally Ringo came to me and said he was working on a project for a series of films that would probably make a TV series. He didn't go ahead with that project in any case,' but the film itself got made. It was good timing because, earlier that year in March when the idea was finalized, Bolan was about to enthral everyone at Wembley and Ringo Starr managed to film both performances. Additional filming was then done at John Lennon's country estate, an airfield in Riply and finally some studio footage, shot with Elton John. Marc made the nature of the film very clear: 'It has absolutely no plot – it's just non-stop rock 'n' roll with studio and live sequences linked by comedy that's a little on the surreal side.'

The movie kicked off with the première at the Oscar One cinema in London's Brewer Street, Soho, on a Thursday evening, 14 December. The press kit, which came in a package of several parts handed out on the night, was put together by Marc and Ringo Starr's press agent. It is reproduced here.

PART ONE: BACKGROUNDER

Born to Boogie is, according to Marc Bolan who stars in it with T.Rex, 'a film with surrealistic overtones'. It is also a film laden with the music of the 'boogie bopper' complex; by that one means, 'It sells on disc' and will surely achieve a carbon 'Black' copy success for this Apple film which is produced, directed by and also stars Ringo Starr. The film is about that which is happening in pop music – NOW! Amongst the fourteen songs (plus a reprise of many) are at least *six Marc Bolan number one hits*. It is not intended as a documentary of our time and moment, but simply an offering to appeal to those youngsters – maybe starting around eleven years and up'ards – who just wish to hear their music, to be catered for, to be able to go to a cinema and see, hear, absorb and enjoy some 65 minutes prepared purely with them in mind. Certainly if the records of Messrs Bolan, Starr, Elton John ... 'and other nuns' is any criteria then they have the formula for success. So – wherever you see *Born to Boogie*, please leave any preconceived ideas outside ... and bring your teenage mentor into the warmth and rapport she or he will feel with this delightful film – made expressly with THEM in mind.

PART TWO: MARC BOLAN SUMMARIZES THE RINGO STARR/APPLE FILM *BORN TO BOOGIE*

The film was made purely as a piece of rock and roll entertainment. I feel it documents the phenomenon that has been T.Rex through the past year – and that was the purpose of the film initially. But as Ringo and I became more involved in the making of *Born to Boogie* we decided to add several more scenes, bringing in 'accidental' humour, and to shoot actually 'live' without dubbing. By so doing we were endeavouring to get a spontaneity which does not come naturally from some films. In some of the scenes outside of the concert we let our imaginations take their course and, with the aid of props and a dwarf, let whichever happened, happen. And it did. We made the film strictly for a teenage audience who demand youthful excitement of the cinema as well as on television and in the theatre. I think the film does that – no more, no less.

PART THREE: *BORN TO BOOGIE* SCORE

COMPOSITION	COMPOSER	PUBLISHER	TIME
MARC'S INTRO	Marc Bolan	Warrior Music Projects Ltd	0.15 secs
'JEEPSTER'	Marc Bolan	Essex Music International Ltd	5.00 secs
'BABY STRANGE'	Marc Bolan	Warrior Music Projects Ltd	4.32 secs

COMPOSITION	COMPOSER	PUBLISHER	TIME
'TUTTI FRUTTI'	Richard Pennyman/ Dorothy La Bostrie	Venice Music Ltd	1.21 secs
'CHILDREN OF THE REVOLUTION'	Marc Bolan	Warrior Music Projects Ltd	3.45 secs
'LOOK TO THE LEFT'	Marc Bolan	Warrior Music Projects Ltd	0.19 secs
'SPACEBALL RICOCHET'	Marc Bolan	Warrior Music Projects Ltd	4.12 secs
'SOME PEOPLE LIKE TO ROCK' (LYRIC EXTRACT **'LET'S HAVE A PARTY'**)	Jessie May Robinson	Carlin Music Corp	0.12 secs
'TELEGRAM SAM'	Marc Bolan	Wizard Artists Ltd	4.11 secs
'SOME PEOPLE LIKE TO ROCK' (LYRIC EXTRACT **'LET'S HAVE A PARTY'**)	Jessie May Robinson	Carlin Music Corp	0.33 secs
'COSMIC DANCER'	Marc Bolan	Essex Music International Ltd	3.51 secs
'SOME PEOPLE LIKE TO ROCK' (LYRIC EXTRACT **'LET'S HAVE A PARTY'**)	Jessie May Robinson	Carlin Music Corp	0.07 secs
'JEEPSTER'	Marc Bolan	Essex Music International Ltd	1.15 secs
'HOT LOVE'	Marc Bolan	Essex Music International Ltd	0.55 secs
'GET IT ON'	Marc Bolan	Essex Music International Ltd	1.37 secs
'THE SLIDER'	Marc Bolan	Wizard Artists Ltd	1.54 secs
'UNION HALL POEM' (SPOKEN WORD)	Marc Bolan	Wizard Artists Ltd	0.15 secs
'HOT LOVE'	Marc Bolan	Essex Music International Ltd	11.20 secs
'CHARIOT CHOOGLE'	Marc Bolan	Wizard Artists Ltd	3.00 secs

PART FOUR: *BORN TO BOOGIE* TECHNICAL/ COLOUR CREDITS

Starring Marc Bolan & T.Rex · **Thanks to** Ringo Starr . Elton John . Mickey Finn . Geoffrey Baildon . George Claydon . Miss Chelita . Mune Light . Hilary Bluebyrd · **Cameramen** Nick Knowland . Richard Starkey . Mike Dodds . Mike Davis . Jeremy Stavenhagen . Richard Stanley · **Track Sound Recordist** Tony Visconti · **Sound Recordist** Tony Jackson · **Track Reductions Engineer** Richard Lowezey/Cine Tele Sound Ltd · **Editor** Graham Gilding · **Music Editor** Gene Ellis · **Effects**

Editor Paul Edmunds · **Assistant Editor** Wendy Bindloss · **Production Secretary** Jaqi Nellist · **Boom Operator** Steven Ransley · **Make Up** Heather Nurse · Yvonne Coppard · Ann Marie Ward · **Assistants** David Strong · Mal Evans · **Opticals and Titles** National Screen Service Ltd · **Production** Tim Van Rellim · **Executive Director** Frank Simon · **Produced and Directed** Ringo Starr

·   ·   ·

As 'Solid Gold' was storming up the charts, Marc announced that he would be playing three special T.Rexmas gigs, one at Edmonton Sundown on 22 December and the other as two houses at the Brixton Sundown on 23 December. The fans rushed to purchase tickets, priced at a keen £1.25, for shows that were quite simply stunning. All the regrets, all the bad feelings at having been deserted melted away the moment Marc Bolan appeared on stage in gold lamé dungarees. The sound was heavier, tighter than ever before, but the excitement had also changed. Yes, there was enthusiasm; yes, the kids were still screaming; but it was tempered by a little reserve, a desire almost not to annoy Marc and send him away again. The sound itself was more soulful and what a showman! Bolan had entered a new era, but would it be enough?

By anyone's standards, 1972 had proved to be a spectacular year. T.Rex had achieved four hit singles of which two, 'Metal Guru' and 'Telegram Sam', were in the Top Ten best-selling singles of the year at numbers eight and ten respectively. Then, to cap this, they were voted best band for the second year running and, while not appearing in the best album category, strangely they appeared at number three as the best-selling album band. This anomaly had a great deal to do with the FLY album releases; somehow it is doubtful that Marc would want to thank them for it. In any case he was flying high himself and did not have too much time or energy to waste on disappointment.

5 · (Whatever Happened to the) Teenage Dream?

For all his stature as a pop musician in the early seventies, it is a surprise that Marc Bolan did not appear more often on television in Britain. Until 1973, Bolan had only been seen on BBC's *Top of the Pops*, which was the only television programme then solely to broadcast popular music. There were other shows around he could have graced, though; after all his début on *Music in the Round* in the spring of 1972 had been well received. Marc Bolan had a spellbinding effect on people with whom he came into contact. He could be aggressive as well as incredibly egotistic, but he could also melt hearts with the most innocent of gazes.

At the end of January 1973, T.Rex appeared on the *Cilla Black Show*, which was screened on the evening of Saturday the 27th. They played a new track, 'Mad Donna', from the forthcoming album *Tanx*, and Marc then sang an acoustic version of 'Life's a Gas' as a duet with Cilla. The duet was gushy, to put it mildly, but the appearance caused a storm of protest from the usual group of killjoys who felt that Marc's sexual gyrations, as they chose to describe his performance during 'Mad Donna', were inappropriate for a Saturday evening show. This had strong echoes of Presley and 1950s' repression.

The fans did not object, though, as it gave them another all to rare glimpse of Bolan and the band. But, if the English fans thought that the appearance of Marc on Cilla Black's show was the beginning of a period of high profile, they were sadly mistaken. In fact, February was spent in Germany and Austria and the English fans were now having to learn to share Marc Bolan. It was not easy; and there were other pop idols who had begun to break through in 1972 and who in 1973 were a serious threat to Marc's status: Gary Glitter, the Sweet and Slade were all to notch up more hit singles than Marc this year.

On 2 March, T.Rex issued their first single of 1973. With advance sales of over 100,000, it was of little surprise that '20th Century Boy' entered the singles chart at a very pleasing number three. The single was fast, furious, aggressive and heavy, the opening power chords sending out a clear message to the gathering band of Bolan knockers who claimed that Marc was finished and that all his songs sounded the same. '20th Century Boy' was kept at number three yet again by Slade

at number one with 'Cum On Feel the Noize' and the American heart-throb, Donny Osmond at number two with the slushy 'Twelfth of Never'.

The same week that T.Rex's single reversed to number five, they released the new album *Tanx*. It went straight in at number four, just as *The Slider* had done the previous year. It then spent a second week at number four, unlike *The Slider*, but thereon slowly reversed, and here any similarity ended. Where *The Slider* had been a slick and sexually aggressive album of pop songs, *Tanx* was polished but much more direct. Bolan chose this album, whether consciously or not, to vent his feelings towards the media as well as to hold in contempt those in authority. Furthermore, sexual overtones were evident, as Marc then turned on the parents of his fans, ridiculing their hypocrisy. As youngsters themselves they had had their own idols; why should the youngsters of this generation suffer? What was the harm in their adulation of Marc and his portrayal of his sexuality?

Marc enjoyed a small rumble of outrage with the cover and advertisement photographs for *Tanx* where he sat astride a tank, the gun barrel of the tank in an upward position closely resembling an erection. Was it deliberate? Probably! A member of the public wrote in to a music-paper letters' page and declared the sight to be: 'Provocative and pornographic. Not content with producing "Teenybopper Trash" for doting hordes of thirteen year olds, he now produces this picture which can only be described as an obscenity.' The letter is especially derisory as the writer states at the beginning: 'Having just been shown the advert for the latest T.Rex LP, *Tanx*, I feel I must voice my anger,' and then shows his true colours when he admits: 'I have not heard the record myself.'

A spokesman for Marc Bolan explained: 'I've never seen an obscene tank in my life, although armoured cars are slightly depraved.'

'The Groover', after its release on 2 June, spent just five weeks in the Top Twenty listings. It peaked at number four on the second week of release and with hindsight, perhaps, Bolan would have been better advised then to have been seen as well as heard. It would have been worth the trouble of arranging even just a few live dates to promote the album. This may have caused security problems, such as those experienced the previous year, but no one was going to find out as T.Rex spent the remaining two weeks of June in Germany recording new material. Perhaps

Lighting check

Electric Warrior in America

Steve Currie, Mickey Finn and Bill Legend in a hotel room on tour in America

Marc and June in a dressing room

Early morning limousine communication – Detroit

Touch down – New York

Airport shopping

Greeting the press

Modelling clothes for the next tour – happy days!

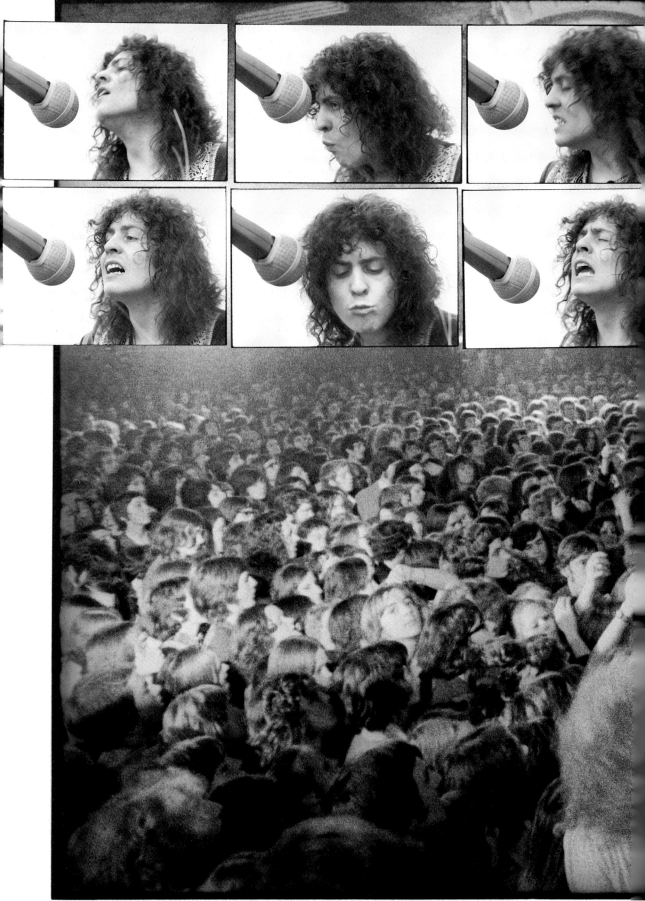

An American gig. *Inset:* Acoustic live for LA radio

New Musical Express relaunch cover session

Rule 1 – Never get too serious

Marc and Mickey press shot

Marc and Mickey – our first session

His granny's fur coat?

On location for *Born to Boogie*

Marc told me he never learnt to drive a car, because he knew one day he'd die in one

Born to Boogie – Apple Studios

Elton John with hair

More from Apple Studios – five minutes with a stuffed tiger produced *The Greatest Hits* cover pic, one of Marc's instant

Duetting on a car roof with Ringo Starr

Left: Eat your heart out Katharine Hepburn!

Dormouse games with Ringo during the making of *Born to Boogie*

Leaving America

Marc was the most visually articulate person I ever photographed,
always knowing how he looked, what shape he made – to say he
was never unaware is an understatement.

For Layla, Lee and Sevrin plus Cathy who was there.

Bolan was becoming scared that the media were right, perhaps he would not need the security, after all, perhaps his star was fading.

While 'The Groover' was spending its brief life in the charts, Bolan and the band took off for Munich to start recording tracks for their next album. Two of the backing singers from the last American tour were invited to Munich to do some backing vocals, as Marc had been immensely impressed by one of the women in particular, and had felt that her 'soul' voice would work well with his new ideas. When Gloria Jones was contacted in America and invited to session again for Marc she was delighted. She approached her friend, who had also appeared on the last T.Rex tour, to join her at Marc's request, only to discover that she was not available. Gloria turned to another close friend whom she had known since childhood: Pat Hall, a southern gospel singer, who fortunately was free to work and the ensuing partnership of these two 'soul sisters' was to knock Marc sideways. The backing sounds they created were unique to T.Rex and musically it worked incredibly well.

The band was also expanding in other ways. Prior to beginning a six-week tour of America in July, Marc Bolan signed up guitarist Jack Green. With Gloria Jones and Pat Hall also invited on the tour, Marc felt, with justified confidence, that the new and live T.Rex were ready for America, but was America ready for them?

The tour was gruelling and Bolan's obsession with America was, in the eyes of many people, his downfall. It took in fifteen dates, starting at Milwaukee on 20 July, and moving from city to city: Chicago, Detroit, Michigan, Memphis, Florida, Kansas, Mississippi, Davenport, Miami, Iowa, Nassau, New York, Santa Monica and Los Angeles. On this tour they were the opening act for Three Dog Night and initially the fans reactions to T.Rex were not encouraging. There was a polite response, but nothing dramatic; however, this did not remain the case. Slowly but surely fans started appearing at the concerts wearing glitter make-up, and Marc Bolan began to get feedback from the crowds. In Memphis the first signs of Rextasy appeared when more than just a few fans got off their seats and danced to the beat. The band were tight. Perhaps Marc's conquest trail of America would work out after all.

After a brief holiday in the Bahamas during September, Bolan and T.Rex spent

October touring first Japan, where they played to packed houses in Tokyo, Nagoya, Hiroshima and Fukuoka, and then Australia, where a four-date mini-tour started at the Hordern Pavilion in Sydney on 3 November. This was followed by appearances at the Apollo Stadium in Adelaide on the 6th, the Festival Hall Melbourne on the 7th, to finish at the Festival Hall in Brisbane on the 10th.

Sadly, while Marc was obviously doing well everywhere else in the world, England was to continue slowly to turn its back on him. The T.Rex Wax Co issued an album titled *T.Rex Great Hits* which was shunned overall by the fans as it became the first T.Rex album not to enter the Top Thirty, although settling only just outside at number thirty-two. 'Truck On (Tyke)' the third single of the year was released on 16 November to derision by the press. Marc had to rely once more on a hard core of fans to chart the single: the initial chart position of number twenty was the lowest in over three years and, worst still, it was the first T.Rex single not to enter the Top Ten chart since 'Magical Moon' in January 1970.

Worse was yet to follow. On the completion of the T.Rex tour of Australia, a spokesman for T.Rex announced that Bill Legend had 'left the band'. Bill's explanation was that he had been on the road with T.Rex for almost three years and his personal life had suffered greatly; quite simply 'the fun and magic had died.' It was a shock to the faithful and reverberated fresh worries about the future, cemented as T.Rex were voted only the sixth best singles band of 1973 in a music-press poll, finishing below Dawn (1), Slade (2), Wizzard (3), the Sweet (4) and the Osmonds (5). They featured in no other categories. Marc Bolan's crown had undoubtedly slipped.

.   .   .

The first two weeks of 1974 opened with the 'Truck On (Tyke)' single floating out of the singles Top Twenty. Bolan announced that T.Rex were to tour the United Kingdom, for the first time since 1972, opening at the Newcastle City Hall on 21 January, followed by the Glasgow Apollo on the 22nd, Sheffield City Hall on the 24th, Manchester City Hall on the 26th, Leicester De Montfort Hall on the 27th and finishing at the Birmingham Odeon on 28 January.

An announcement was also made of the new T.Rex line-up. Mickey Finn

(percussion) and Steve Currie (bass) had been joined by Jack Green (guitar) during the summer of 1973, but had not yet been seen by English fans. Gloria Jones and Pat Hall were also to be introduced to English audiences, as well as the exciting addition of two drummers, Davey Lutton and Paul Felton. The final surprise came in the shape of two saxophonists. The fans were in for a treat as the new line-up gave T.Rex a much heavier and fuller sound and the driving beat supplied by the two drummers was quite incredible. Davey Lutton's previous experience with Joe Cocker's backing band linked in well with former Carmen drummer, Paul Felton.

The Glasgow Apollo gig, the second on the tour, opened with the strangest support band imaginable: Chilli Willie, who played a set consisting of country music and old swing and found themselves fighting, as others had before them, to be heard against the chants of 'Bolan, Bolan'. The Chilli Willie set complete, the audience awaited the first glimpse of Marc on stage for two years. As the backdrop heralded the arrival of T.Rex in massive flashing lights, the glitter had all but gone, and a much heavier Bolan emerged on stage, to a tremendous welcome. The band launched themselves into '20th Century Boy', to be greeted by a huge bellow of appreciation, a sound much like the collapse of a brick wall. 'The Groover', 'Jeepster', 'Telegram Sam', 'Metal Guru', 'Hot Love' and 'Get It On', all were pounded out to a loyal gathering, while the new single 'Teenage Dream' was greeted with caution. The fans had been trapped in a time warp and found this new, slower mood somewhat disconcerting.

'(Whatever Happened to the) Teenage Dream', the first single of the year was released on 26 January 1973, appearing in the charts to arrive at the disappointingly low number eighteen. It was to be Marc Bolan's only Top Twenty hit out of three attempts in 1974 and, sadly for his fans, the title evoked a bitter twist of irony. Watching a bloated performance on *Top of the Pops* the week the single peaked at number thirteen, one could not help but ask that very question: what had happened to our Teenage Dream? It seemed that drugs and drink had taken their toll of the once beautiful, elfin face of rock. It was to be a while before the Bolan of old was to re-emerge, by which time, it was almost too late.

All that said, musically Marc Bolan had matured a great deal, as indeed had many of his fans. The pop-star image of 1972–3 was a phase through which he had

passed and while he had enjoyed that period, what was happening for him now was much more important. Marc himself was to say that he had got far too mixed up in the David Cassidy/Donny Osmond syndrome of teenybopper adulation. 'Any rock star can do that' was his response to the period. Life itself meant much more to the new Marc Bolan; he had never been so free to be himself and get back to enjoying his music. 'Teenage Dream', in his opinion, was lyrically the best single, he had ever recorded. 'I'm proud of it. Unintentionally, it's very different.'

Without a shadow of a doubt 'Teenage Dream' was different; the concept very mellow and outward looking. The strings were stunning, reportedly a forty-piece orchestra with beautiful piano accompaniment, played by Lonnie Jordan of the band, War. Far removed from white swans, magical moons and metal gurus, the new album was awaited eagerly. The final change was to the band's title. By Marc's own admission, T.Rex was no more. What he now had was a solo career with a great bunch of musicians and the official band title became: Marc Bolan and T.Rex as Zinc Alloy & the Hidden Riders of Tomorrow. Supposedly, this was to give Marc the scope to bring in changes, as and when he felt them worthy, without confusing his fans. A rerun of the uncertainty surrounding the band's survival in 1969 when Tyrannosaurus Rex lost Steve Took was not to be allowed to happen again.

On the first day of February *Zinc Alloy and the Hidden Riders of Tomorrow: A Creamed Cage in August* was issued. A little-known fact is that, although when released the album was accredited to Marc Bolan and T.Rex, and the title was as given, this was not as Bolan had planned it. When the album artwork was first delivered to EMI, the names of neither Marc Bolan nor T.Rex were anywhere to be seen. The artwork was innovative for its time: a cream-coloured sleeve with an interwoven photograph of Marc in its centre and the words on the cover Zinc Alloy & the Hidden Riders of Tomorrow were written in a flowing ink-pen style. The sleeve then opened upwards and to either side, each movement taking a little of the image of Bolan with it finally to reveal an airbrushed portrait of his face. In the bottom right-hand corner, in the same style as the name, was the title: 'A Creamed Cage in August'.

The name, Zinc Alloy, was meant to be Marc Bolan's alter ego. It came from

years earlier when Marc had jokingly told a reporter
would change his name to Zinc Alloy and wear an
was attempting to do just that. EMI were horrified;
that this would be nothing short of suicide, as it had
it was to sell a T.Rex product to a sceptical public.
one, but two changes. The first was that the names
appear on the front of the sleeve, ending up as a red
rner, and the second involved a limit to the run of
s far as EMI were concerned, such lavish presentation
urrent paper shortage, due to the Arab embargo on
pop-up sleeve therefore became a specially numbered
which it would revert to the usual gatefold design.
ted by the press and the fans, on the whole, seemed
nt as sales were disappointing. This was a shame
tly produced by Marc Bolan and Tony Visconti,
of which many deserve the label, progressive. The
mongst the classic Bolan offerings, and it is a shame
more respect amongst fellow musicians, the public,
ns, had become distinctly unimpressed. The album
peaked at number twelve, the lowest album chart position in over four years.

More shocks were in store for the Bolan faithful with the news at the beginning
of March of Tony Visconti's departure. It was announced that he was 'with
regret' leaving the T.Rex stable after nearly six years of musical association. The
announcement was met with as much horror by Marc's fans as if he had been a
member of the band. In a way, though, it was as if a member of the band had left,
for to a great many people, Tony Visconti was the fifth member of T.Rex. The
reasons for the split were acknowledged as 'musical differences', but in reality it
was yet another sign of a crumbling era. In *The Record Producers* Tony Visconti
explained that the formula of the T.Rex sound really had not changed since 1971
when 'Get It On' was recorded: 'I could wake up in the middle of the night and
set up a Marc Bolan sound for you on the desk, or a Marc Bolan mix, within five
minutes.'

'The Children of Rarn' suite was a Bolan project close to Tony Visconti's heart. It was meant to have been a concept album in its own right. The original idea was that of a musical version of something similar to Tolkien's *Lord of the Rings*, where a young man becomes the saviour of a mythical world called Rarn, narrating the classic fight of good against evil. The hint of its eventual release was on the opening and closing sequences of the 1970 *T.Rex* album. Since then, each time Bolan went into the studios, Visconti would ask him whether the new album would be 'The Children of Rarn', and Marc would say yes and then promptly abandon the idea as soon as he started recording. Finally Visconti lost patience when the promised 'Children of Rarn' concept was shoved aside for *Zinc Alloy* and handed in his notice at the end of the *Zinc Alloy* sessions.

'I just handed in my notice,' he explained. 'I never thought "The Children of Rarn" was going to materialize, and, in fact, it never did [during Marc's lifetime].' Tony Visconti counted himself rightly as one of Bolan's closest friends and the split upset him greatly. Had Bolan lived it is almost certain that he and Visconti would have worked together again. In the realm speculation that may be, but in reality Bolan did manage to carry on without Tony Visconti. In an interview much later in the year he said of the split with Visconti: *It kind of happened on its own. I wasn't happy with what was coming out of the relationship towards the end. It gets to the point where you have learned all there is to learn from someone. Tony is a folk producer really and he wasn't energizing me any more. I can energize myself very easily ... I'm a fucking good producer. It doesn't matter whose name is on the album cover, just as long as the sound is coming out right. It was ceasing to sound the way I wanted it to. I began to realize that it wasn't urgent enough.'*

On 13 July 'Light of Love' was released and the dying embers of support for Marc Bolan allowed the single to reach a low-profile number twenty-two. The band line-up had changed yet again, with the loss of Paul Fenton and Pat Hall and the arrival of Dino Dines, a keyboard player. Recorded in Los Angeles, the sounds were distinctly American-orientated, the beat solid enough with a sprinkling of funk. Sadly, it did not match up to the spirited change that Marc had so confidently pioneered during the *Zinc Alloy* sessions and the 'Teenage Dream' sound. This

constant change in direction, as it clearly was, proved partly to blame for Marc's fall from grace, and increased his insecurity, making it appear that he was chasing his own tail.

Bolan left England for the shores of America once more in the summer of 1974. Gloria Jones, by this time publicly known as his partner both musically and personally, went with him. The split with June Bolan had actually occurred at the tailend of 1973, with Gloria being cited as the 'other party' in the subsequent divorce proceedings. Marc needed to be in the States because there were details of a projected tour to be finalized, as well as a new recording deal to be struck, as the existing contract with the American giants, Warner Brothers, with whom Marc had been for some three years, was about to finish.

The 1974 tour of America started on 26 September, with the first two gigs in Pennsylvania on the 26th at the Tower Theatre in Upper Darby and on the 28th at Johnstown. The bill was shared with the Blue Oyster Cult. Moving on to a club called Joint in the Woods, Parsippany, in New Jersey, on 2 October, T.Rex appeared on the late evening spot to give the East Coast fans a taste of new material, including 'Solid Baby', 'Precious Star', 'Zip Gun Boogie' and 'Token of My Love', at that time all of which were unreleased tracks. They also treated the audience to some oldies such as 'Jeepster', 'Get It On' ('Bang a Gong') and 'Telegram Sam'.

There followed a gap of some four weeks before Marc Bolan and the band were seen gigging again. Natalie McDonald, who published, along with several fellow American Bolan fans, a quite brilliant fanzine titled *Electric Warrior*, reported in issue three that Marc had fallen ill and had had to cancel several dates in California and one in New York.

While Marc was about to get back on the road in the States, in England the T.Rex Wax Co released 'Zip Gun Boogie' backed with 'Space Boss'. It spluttered at number forty-one, and with it the humiliation was surely complete. Marc was later to blame 'mistiming' as one of the reasons for his first real flop since becoming a rock star. He was getting even closer when he admitted that the lack of promotion was also responsible, but he attempted to shrug it off by listing the failures of John Lennon and Stevie Wonder as well as his own: 'You can't put records out with no promotion, and at the wrong time of year,' he explained and with that famous

impish grin concluded, 'Still, at least I flopped in good company.'

Meanwhile, back in America, on 9 November Bolan and T.Rex appeared at the Roberts Stadium in Evansville, Indiana. Guess Who, a band with a minor hit in England in 1970 with 'American Woman', also appeared on the bill. Next stop was the Agora Club, in Cleveland, Ohio on 11 November, where the gig was broadcast live on a local radio station and the support band was Carmen, the band with whom Paul Fenton had been the drummer before joining T.Rex. Four days later T.Rex appeared alongside the Sensational Alex Harvey Band at the Trenton War Memorial Theatre in Trenton, New Jersey on 15 November and on the following day they were support to ZZ Top at the Capitol Theatre, Port Chester, New York. The tour ended at the St Moritz Hotel, New York City on 17 November.

The year ended with the announcement in the press that Bolan was quitting England for tax reasons and would be residing in Los Angeles. He also talked for the first time about his split with June Feld, his lover, his wife and, not acknowledged at the time, the driving force behind his success between 1969 and 1973. 'We just grew apart,' was his admission to Jan Iles in the *Record Mirror*. 'We couldn't relate to each other any more. Plus I was away most of the time. I guess it's very hard being the wife of a rock star.' Later on in the article he added, 'We're still good friends, I mean I never considered myself married in the first place.'

For June, the affair with Gloria had been the last straw. In an interview with Danae Brook of the London *Evening News*, she said of Marc, 'I knew what he was like when he was in love because it was just like we used to be. When I found out about Gloria I just could not take it in again. It was too painful.' June continued: 'You see, it was the third time he'd had an affair. He couldn't just go off and have a quick scene. He had to fall in love. I'd been through it twice already; once it was another singer, once a painter, and I knew the signs.'

·   ·   ·

Very little of note happened in 1975, but T.Rex continued to make music. *Bolan's Zip Gun* was released on 16 February, and Marc's concept of the album appeared to be totally different from public expectations. The tracks were, quite simply, too far removed from what the fans had hoped for and wanted. Yet Marc himself said

of *Bolan's Zip Gun*: 'It's definitely the nearest thing I've done to *Electric Warrior*. It's very commercial, a kinda rock'n'roller.' But, the majority of the fans gave up, and ignored the album, reflected in poor sales and little acclaim: there was nothing left of the Bolan of 1971–3, and this was a bitter pill to swallow. What is ironic is that *Bolan's Zip Gun* has now become another classic, and, with a couple of appalling exceptions, there are many excellent tracks, such as 'Solid Baby', 'Precious Star', 'Think Zinc' and the quite stunning 'Till Dawn'. All of them were way ahead of their time. While appreciating with hindsight Marc's feelings about this album, it was by far the most difficult album to pinpoint and label. This inability to home in on its character explains the fans' confusion and subsequent cool reception.

When an announcement was made that Mickey Finn was to leave T.Rex, many felt that the band were finished for good. Unlike the loss of Bill Legend and to a certain degree, Tony Visconti, Mickey's departure was seen as the break-up of the very heart of T.Rex, and with good reason. Mickey Finn had been a part of the set up from the near beginning and to a great extent was as synonymous with T.Rex as Marc himself. Mickey Finn's leaving has never been fully explained and until now has remained in the realms of pure speculation. Recently, though, he has broken his years of silence in an interview reproduced here in chapter six, 'Reflections'.

Bolan, for his part, was in no mood to linger in the past and announced that a new T.Rex line-up would be arriving in England during July to do a few selected gigs. Shortly afterwards came the release of the first new single of the year on 21 June, which quite inexplicably put T.Rex back in the Top Twenty charts with 'New York City'. There it remained for eight weeks, peaking at number fifteen.

The new line-up was to be Steve Currie (bass) Davey Lutton (drums) Gloria Jones (clavinet and backing vocals) Dino Dines (keyboards) and Tyrone Scott (keyboards and backing vocals) and the mini tour seen as a warm-up for the next full-scale British tour to be announced in the autumn. The band were billed as T.Rex and the 'ballroom' dates were held at the Palace Lido on the Isle of Man, Sunday, 12 July, followed by Tiffany's in Great Yarmouth on the 23rd, the Pier Pavilion on the 25th, and finally the Leas Cliff Hall on the 26th. Marc's explanation to the press about such minor venues was greeted with a degree of smugness by

the media: 'We just want to play non-prestige dates, and renew our acquaintance with record buyers. We don't want to get involved in larger concerts'. He was later to confess, in an interview with Chris Welch for *Melody Maker* that: *I did those four crazy ballroom gigs a couple of months ago, with no promotion, just to see how things were. 'Would they just sit there and look at me?' I didn't know. And they sold out, and the response was amazing, with no publicity. The local kids just turned out. And it went down well. But it could have bombed, and we wanted to bomb in secret.*

September 1975 saw the birth of Rolan, Marc's first and only child, a son by his girlfriend Gloria Jones. Bolan held a press call and announced proudly that he had been there at the birth. Coincidently, on the very day that Rolan was born, on 26 September, Marc released his second and last single of 1975: 'Dreamy Lady' by the T.Rex Disco Party. It enjoyed limited success, reaching number thirty in the single charts.

.   .   .

In January 1976 Marc Bolan announced the biggest T.Rex tour in England since the *Electric Warrior* concerts in autumn 1971. Between 5 February and 6 March, they would appear at no less than seventeen venues.

The first major gig in the United Kingdom for two years kicked off at the Central Hall in Chatham, Kent, on 5 February, followed by City Hall, St Albans on the 6th, Leas Cliffe Hall, Folkestone on the 7th, Cliffe's Pavilion in Southend on the 8th, the Floral Hall in Southport on the 12th, the Palace Theatre, Newark on the 13th, the Grand Pavilion in Witherensea on St Valentine's Day, Empire Theatre, Sunderland on the 15th, the Lyceum in London on the 18th, the Queensway, Dunstable on the 19th. On the 20th, T.Rex appeared again at the Winter Gardens in Bournemouth, the place where T.Rextasy had begun all those years ago before in 1971. This was followed by a further series of gigs: on the 23rd at Birmingham Town Hall, the Manchester Free Trade Hall on the 24th, the Winter Gardens at New Brighton on the last day of February. Scotland got its turn in the first week of March when the Glasgow Apollo greeted T.Rex on the 1st, the

Municipal Hall at Falkirk on the 3rd, the Civic Centre, Motherwell on the 4th and finally the Grand Hall at Kilmarnock.

The tour went under the banner of the *Futuristic Dragon*, which was the title of the brand new album to be released on 31 January. There were early signs of a reversal in the chart fortunes of T.Rex when the album was listed in the Top Fifty, albeit only at number fifty. The initial optimism was dashed, however, when the album disappeared out of the charts and sank without trace.

The tour by this time was under way and there was a groundswell of support once more but it was not sufficient to improve the chart position of the album. Nevertheless the tour had its moments and the two major highlights were Manchester and Glasgow, areas where Marc's support had always been strong. On 21 February 1976, midway through the tour, 'London Boys', the new single was released. Given the revived high profile of the band, and the quality of the single it should have done better than its poor final position of number forty in the singles charts, but its weak performance served some purpose at least. It was at the end of the tour that Marc decided to take a long hard look at himself. As a result, some of the old fighting spirit returned.

Released on 5 June, 'I Love to Boogie' was the fourteenth T.Rex single. It took four weeks from its release before it appeared out of nowhere at seventeen in the singles chart. It was not without controversy as Marc was accused of unashamedly copying an old fifties number when rock 'n' roll fans claimed that 'I Love to Boogie' was a blatant rip-off of Webb Pierce's 1956 rockabilly recording 'Teenage Boogie'. Disc jockey, Geoff Barker, was quoted in the music press as saying, 'The records are so alike it can't be coincidence. He's kept the basic melody, and simply changed the chorus lyrics. Even the guitar solo is a rip-off.' Oldies purists met at the Castle in the Old Kent Road where, with great ceremony, they burnt a copy of Marc's single. Bolan stayed strangely quiet throughout the controversy.

The week after its release, 'I Love to Boogie' slipped down a place, only to recover the week after and, at number thirteen, give Marc his biggest hit single in over two years. It was also, sadly, the last during his lifetime.

By the time the final single of 1976 was released on 17 September, Marc had

changed the line-up of T.Rex for the eighth time since the band's inception and the fifth time since the end of 1973. Miller Anderson (guitar) became the latest recruit and with his input, they produced 'Laser Love', a slick but uncharacteristically heavy number that continues to confuse fans to this day. Equally disorienting was his performance on *Top of the Pops* (in the days when established artistes got to air their new singles), when he appeared with a brand-new image. Dressed in a suit and tie, it was the hairstyle that came as a shock: the curls cut off and the hair slicked back, Bolantino made his début.

In December 1976 Marc Bolan and T.Rex took part in a live television special to be screened over the Christmas period. Special guests were the heavy-metal band AC/DC and the show was called *The Rollin' Bolan Show*. A very healthy Bolan, possibly looking his best since 1973, graced the screen. He had a renewed confidence about him that bode well not only for his own future, but also for fans, who had thought the days of their idol were not just numbered, but over.

The sad note at the end of the year was the decision of Steve Currie to leave T.Rex. Unlikely though it may seem, it was actually Steve who had been the longest serving member of T.Rex, not, as many believed, Mickey Finn. Davey Lutton also moved on but not by his own initiative. Bolan wanted to change the feel of T.Rex and Lutton did not fit into his plans. By all accounts, he did not take his dismissal lightly.

.   .   .

The ninth and final T.Rex line-up was announced in January 1977: Miller Anderson (guitar), Dino Dines (keyboards), Herbie Fowers (bass), Tony Newman (drums) and Alfa Alfa (backing vocals). Along with these cast changes came a new album, *Dandy in the Underworld*; with its arrival a breath of fresh air was blown into the concept of T.Rex. Gone was the ego, kicked into touch the overindulgent production. Marc Bolan had returned to basics, good old cosmic rock, and the sounds, while not so highly polished, were reminiscent of *Electric Warrior*. The album sold well, but never in sufficient numbers to reach high into the UK album charts.

The *Dandy in the Underworld* tour, which began on 10 March, was to be the last of Marc Bolan's career. Wittingly or not, Bolan had made a shrewd move when

he decided to take as support an up and coming punk band. The inclusion of the Damned guaranteed a new following, as their fans were in turn to get hooked on Marc, and Bolan allowed a little of his ego to creep in when he described himself, tongue in cheek, as the father of punk. His crowning glory came at the Rainbow Theatre in London's Finsbury Park. His performance there brought back good memories; for everyone it was a night to savour. The tour had started on 10 March at the City Hall, Newcastle, followed by Manchester Apollo on the 11th, Glasgow Apollo on the 12th, Victoria Hall, Hanley on the 13th, Colston Hall, Bristol on the 14th, Birmingham Odeon on the 17th, the Rainbow, London, on the 18th, the Pavilion, West Runton on the 19th, to end at the Lacarno in Portsmouth on the 20th.

On 30 May the title track from the album was released as a single, its mix different from that of the album, with some of the words changed to eliminate the reference to cocaine on the earlier version. Someone had got cold feet. There was also the much welcomed return to the two-title flip side, missing from T.Rex singles since 'Children of the Revolution' in 1972 and 'Dreamy Lady' in 1975.

August 1977 will be best remembered for the start of a six-part series made for Granada television, *The Marc Shows*, which Bolan hosted and appeared on with his band. First screening was Wednesday, 24 August at 4.45 p.m. The idea was to introduce new pop-music acts, as well as to provide visiting star slots for established artists; there was also a regular airing of T.Rex material. Amongst those who were first seen on this series were Billy Idol with Generation X, the Boomtown Rats and the Jam. Marc was also to pull off a major coup when David Bowie agreed to appear on the sixth show in the series. It had been three years since Bowie had last appeared on British television and the highlight of the show was a jam session at the end, with the two rock stars vying for the crowded space on stage.

Marc, however, was never to see this show, or indeed the one that preceded it. By the time the last two shows were screened, the world for many had been torn apart. In the early hours of Friday, 16 September, Marc Bolan and Gloria Jones were heading home in their purple Mini. At a notorious blackspot on Gypsy Lane, Barnes Common, with Gloria Jones behind the wheel, the car left the road and crashed into a tree. Marc, just two weeks short of his thirtieth birthday, died instantly.

6 · Reflections

In the first few years following the tragic early death of Marc Bolan, his memory was only kept alive by a comparatively small number of fans. Various fanzines sprang up and enjoyed limited success due to a thirst for knowledge about Marc, or more importantly, a need for togetherness. It is sometimes incredibly difficult to explain to casual observers just what impact Marc Bolan had had on the lives of his fans.

Quite rightly, the focus of sympathy at the time was on Marc Bolan's family. Simeon and Phyllis Feld had a great deal contend with and, to their credit, they coped extremely well. The continuous coming and going of fans to the flat in south London where they lived was endless and at times they were close to breaking point. They were never really given the space that would have allowed time to heal the loss of their son. Sadly both of Marc's parents died in 1991.

For Harry Feld, Marc's half-brother, the years following Marc's death have been frustrated by a catalogue of his stolen effects being sold at auction. The most disgusting example of this was a retired mortuary assistant's attempts to sell the blood-stained clothes in which Marc had died. Thankfully, Harry was able to retrieve the items of clothing and have them burnt publicly at his home in Portsmouth in front of members of the press. But, there have been many other genuine items of memorabilia that have been preserved, such as guitars, original handwritten manuscripts, stage clothes and autographs, all of which have seen the light of day at auctions over the years. No one objects to this as their sale does no harm and the goods were, on the whole, legally obtained.

·   ·   ·

For Gloria Jones, September 1977 was obviously devastating and she moved quite quickly back to America, where she now resides in Los Angeles with Rolan, her son by Bolan. For Gloria, at least, there is some comfort, some lasting evidence of her life with Marc Bolan, in the shape of Rolan, who, in 1992, the fifteenth anniversary year of his death, will be sixteen years old. Gloria has much to say on her life with Marc and the following extract is an edited version of the article that

appeared in the international official fan club magazine *Rarn* in December 1985, written by the authors on a visit to Gloria Jones in America.

The very first thing we were to discover was that Gloria and time-keeping did not, and do not, go well together! Our arrival in Los Angeles had been bewildering with a whirlwind tour of the city straight from the airport. The night had been planned as a quick chat and early to bed for two travel-worn people, but Gloria had other plans and we did not say goodnight until nearly 4 a.m. What seemed even more cruel was that we had then to rise and be ready for an exciting day with Gloria, starting at 9.30 the following morning.

Eleven o'clock saw the arrival in the hotel foyer of a radiant Gloria Jones who confessed to having slept only a little since our departure a few hours before. 'OK, you guys, the first stop is my house to meet my mom and pop.' The next thing we discovered about Gloria was that she never goes in a straight line anywhere! To travel to her house (a couple of miles from where we were staying in Hollywood), we must have detoured to add an extra fifteen to twenty miles to the journey. On the way to her parents' house Gloria stopped at some of the grandest looking houses imaginable; the first was the residence of one Miss Diana Ross, and we were terrified, on learning that Gloria knew her, that we were going to get invited in for a cup of coffee. This was followed by what was for us the most amazing residential building of all in Los Angeles, which turned out to be the home of the mayor. It was so large and security conscious as to be stage managed. We decided to split fast when the security men at the gate began to take an interest in our car parked outside and opposite, fearing that an explanation of our status as English sightseers might have taken a little while.

So, finally, we arrived at Gloria's parents' house, having until then said hardly a word about the man we really wanted to discuss. We were sure that Gloria would open up in her own good time and, to be honest, we were just getting to know each other; we knew that gradually she would begin to talk about Marc. As we were going into the house Gloria turned and said,

'Before we owned our own house, this was our retreat, whenever Marc got over to LA he would head here first.' Neither of us could express what we were

expecting to find on entering the house. There was a feeling, almost a demand, that it should be full of memories, indeed it seemed impossible that there would not be thousands of photographs hanging from walls and a side board with several rows of framed pictures. But, our illusions were dashed, our minds totally unprepared for the sight that was to greet us: one 10×8-inch black and white print of Marc on a coffee table and that, it seemed, had been hard earned.

'The problem was', whispered Gloria, 'that our life was in London. The morning of the car crash the so-called fans ran amok through our house.' The subject was one of obvious emotion to Gloria and it was hard to find the right words to respond.

'It's all right,' Gloria continued, 'there comes a time when you gotta say what you feel and I really feel in my heart that you guys will make sure the truth is told. The people who cleaned out our house left nothing untouched, they even took my clothes. All my Marc's personal and private papers were taken, receipts, letters – Good God, even his American Express dockets were gathered up and sold.'

In response to our next and obvious question about her feelings towards those people, Gloria replied with one word: pity.

'I mean, what kind of person does that to anyone? Let alone the man many of them claimed to love.' Gloria seemed then to go into a world of her own and we all sat very still, as no one, it seemed, wanted to break the train of thought; it seemed like an eternity before Gloria snapped back into life with the comment,

'What is the point of being bitter, those kind of feelings will not change anything now, will they? My life has been empty since Marc, but I have to get on with living for the sake of Rolan and, believe me, I get great strength from knowing that a part of Marc will always be with me through my son.'

'Do you think Rolan had any other effect on Marc, I mean apart from the obvious pride of parenthood?' we asked.

'Sure he did,' replied Gloria. 'My God, that man would have begged, borrowed or stole for Rolan.'

We decided to expand a little on what we meant: 'Was it more than just coincidence that Marc's songs seemed to grow stronger again? Was it not strange that "I Love to Boogie" seemed to scream out with a vitality previously lacking?'

Gloria looked slightly surprised that we could link the two so convincingly.

' "I Love to Boogie" was written for Rolan. Marc said to me, "This is dedicated to Rolan" – you could see the intense emotion in Marc's face when talking about his son.'

Our next question went deeper still, on a subject we ourselves had always needed an answer to for more personal reasons. 'Why did Marc desert England?' There followed a few minutes of silence, then:

'If Marc had any faults at all they were impatience and, more critical than that, he trusted everyone.' It became clear that Gloria was being careful not to set herself up as a target of abuse, knowing that we were going to write about her in *Rarn*, and hopefully would not leave her exposed to criticism due to misunderstanding.

'Marc was too easily swayed by those people who came across as only concerned for him.' Gloria elaborated on this by saying that 'The USA was always a touchy subject with Marc, and his ego found it impossible to accept that America was not at his feet. His head became filled by people who told him the only way to conquer that country was to live and be seen there. Of course, with Marc it would not be quite so easy; his concern was that he did not want to desert his English fans. Marc loved LA, he spent so much time at Malibu beach and the Santa Monica pier – yet his heart was always in England.'

Gloria explained further how 'Marc decided that we should buy a house in England first, but at the same time look for a house on the Californian coast. "That way", Marc told me, "we can have the best of both worlds." I certainly wasn't going to argue with that. Marc asked Tony Howard [Marc's business affairs manager] to start looking for a house in London and it was not long before he found exactly what Marc wanted. The house was a lovely two-storey place with a walled front garden. It was a typical Victorian building, but, my God, did it need redecorating. Marc got to a stage where he went wild with the amount of time it was taking to re-do and in the meantime we were living in a suite at the Portobello Hotel.'

Gloria smiled at the memory of Marc's irritation with the delays. 'The living room was the only one ready when Marc decided we should move in anyway. The

smell of the fresh paint was still very powerful but it was home. The bed was set up in the middle and Marc would sit cross-legged on this bed while all around him chaos reigned with painters and decorators doing the work, somewhat amazed at the man, who had set glam rock on its feet, writing new songs. I believe they really got a kick out of it.'

Later on in the interview Gloria spoke about her pregnancy and the birth of Rolan. 'Marc was so highly strung about Rolan's birth – you would have thought it was him getting fat and finding clothes were not fitting anymore and life could be just a little tense.' Gloria laughed out loud at a memory, 'I had a couple of false alarms, you know. The first time it happened Marc screamed blue murder for people to get to me. I really do believe that the extra pressure of forthcoming parenthood was making Marc a much more mature person.' Gloria ended the interview with a chilling reflection: 'You know, Marc knew he would not see Rolan's second birthday. I remember feeling very cold and being very annoyed and upset with him for having said such a thing – more then because I believed Marc could see into his own future, as I still believe now.'

. . .

Bill Legend has many happy memories of his time with T.Rex. In an interview with us in the summer of 1991, though, it was in telling us about Marc's death and the charade of the funeral that his reflections became fuelled with passion and anger.

'I was working as a freelance illustrator in 1977 when a colleague showed me the newspaper headlines. I found it totally unbelievable, unreal in the true sense of the word. I must admit I had seen the newspaper boards screaming out that a pop star had been killed in a car crash, but not for a single moment did it occur to me that it was anyone I knew, let alone Marc.'

Of the funeral Bill had only distaste to report as he described how 'People arrived dressed up as pop stars, whether they were or weren't.' One particular 'star' arrived at Golders Green Crematorium in his limo, which drew up at the front entrance for maximum effect, 'with a bunch of minders', Bill remembers. 'It was well out of order – you know – it's totally disrespectful. I just sort of dropped

back in the crowd and I could see all this happening. I think it was up to each person to pay their respects and I'm sure they did. Unfortunately there were those that used it for their own advantage.'

For Bill Legend, the chance to work with T.Rex had come as a bit of a shock. 'When Tony Visconti asked me about joining T.Rex I remember being fairly laid back about it saying, "Well, yeah, I'll give it a go – no problems." I was aware of their new-found success as far as "Ride a White Swan" was concerned and', Legend starts laughing, 'I did go out and buy some of the early stuff as I just wanted to familiarize myself. I took it from there.'

The first meeting with Marc was at Air Studios in London, where they met to session. 'Marc was pretty relaxed,' Bill remembers. 'He was sitting behind the desk and getting his sound together. We just shook hands – he was pretty friendly – and we really didn't hang around long, just went into the studio booth and started playing.'

Of Marc's partner, Mickey Finn, Bill recalls from that first session, 'I didn't see him – no, that's not true, I suppose he was there but I was concentrating on the song itself, getting it together. I had obviously said hello to Steve Currie and I felt pretty much at home. The first tracks we recorded were "Hot Love" and "Woodland Rock", the guys made it pretty easy to feel part of the set-up.'

Bill Legend is acknowledged perhaps as being the serious side of T.Rex; indeed, he treated all that he did with dignity and never felt that it was all a game. 'I take it very seriously and it is the same with anything I do, I give it my best. Even now I find when I'm playing a gig that I treat it as if I'm recording a track that goes down for all time and it was just the same then. It really is a question of disciplining yourself and putting the best you can into it."

On touring? 'I wondered where I was sometimes, but that in itself was an amazing experience. After I had joined the band on a permanent basis, following the recording of "Hot Love", I remember going down to the studio in Shaftesbury Avenue where we went through a set and within two weeks I did my first gig with T.Rex – in Detroit!'

Talking about America the subject turned to why Bill thought Marc had never succeeded there. 'I feel that the band did crack the States in a great many places,

but because America is so huge ...' Bill stopped to ponder for a while before continuing, 'I don't know what the audiences were expecting over there – we were so new, with the glam thing and one thing and another – I really don't think they quite knew how to take us.'

Of Marc's obsession with America? 'I think there was always a challenge. Whenever things weren't going quite right there would be a tension, and if we could have relaxed a bit more I think it might have helped Marc. Marc kept himself to himself a lot in America but we did a great deal of recording over there as well – for me that was the highlight, I loved recording a great deal.'

When it came to recording Bill found himself remembering all the frustrations of working with Marc in the studios. 'I felt I had a lot to offer and I liked to give Marc my best, but he was so quick in the studios. He was impatient to get on all the time, whereas I would want to get things right. I would do a piece and say to Marc, on hearing it through, "What if I was to go back?" or "I've got some more ideas."

'"No, no," Marc would say, "that's fine – you've done that three times already!" And as for some of our backing tracks, well you can ask Mickey Finn, he'll vouch for me, we used to do some of them in one take, simply because Marc was so impatient.'

Even though working with Marc in the studios could be very frustrating for Bill he also recognized that for Marc there were goals: 'Marc was a very hard worker in the recording studios, he really loved what he was doing and he really loved to do as much of the work as he could by himself. He was untiring and you got sucked into that feeling, even when you felt that Marc was not letting you be creative, the buzz was there.'

Was the energy and 'live' feel of albums such as the *Electric Warrior* very deliberate? 'Oh, yes,' Bill replied. 'We got the basic tracks done and then the overdubs followed and afterwards double-tracking of drums, voices, guitar and gradual build-up gave the tracks a very live, raunchy rock sound, very, very, very tight as well.'

Bill Legend's personal favourite T.Rex album is *Electric Warrior*: 'It was a wonderful album to play on and the songs ... such great songs. Nice laid-back

feelings, everyone was totally relaxed and everybody was happy with everything.' Bill then gave his own reasons why *Electric Warrior* was so good for him.

'I think it portrayed a very good, successful period – and a very relaxed period, which is something that I think was lacking in later years. Although I do believe that *The Slider* was a very good album as well – probably rather underrated. In actual fact it's one album that I play a lot, even now.'

Whereas *Electric Warrior* was fun and *The Slider* had a certain maturity, by the time *Zinc Alloy* surfaced the happy-go-lucky approach seemed to have disappeared. 'Yeah, I certainly noticed a change. The strange thing about those albums, including *Tanx*, is that I like them all in their own ways,' Bill explains. 'The album *Tanx* for me is very melodic and *Zinc Alloy* was a little more on the funky side, but there was a state of confusion – a non-directional sort of feel to it. Tracks were cut too short in some cases and in others the lack of discipline allowed them to go on for too long.'

Did Bill feel that Tony Visconti's role and subsequent retreat during and after *Zinc Alloy* was a key factor in this? 'I think, in all honesty, if Marc had left people to do the work they were there to do and he had concentrated on what he could do best, then it would have carried on for a longer period of time. I think he began to get too involved in different aspects and tried to do too much himself – he couldn't delegate any more – and I think it told in the end.'

Bill Legend left the band at the end of 1973. Did he ever regret leaving? Did he ever keep tabs on Marc and the others? 'I wonder whether Marc ever really realized that we were all friends. We could all have helped him but it was as if he really didn't want our opinions half the time. We were just there to do a job – you did your job and that was it – that's really how it got to me. I had to get out ... I had a family that I wasn't even seeing grow up and in the end I had quite simply had enough of it all. There were more important things in life and I really did not want to miss out on them. Sadly, I saw no one again until the funeral.'

.   .   .

Mickey Finn and his historical importance to the T.Rex phenomenon is well documented in earlier chapters, but the Mickey Finn we met and interviewed in

the summer of 1991 was but a shadow of his former self, except for the devilish glint in his eye, and a sense of humour that at times was as sharp as any blade, but could turn humble and blunt in an instant. Strangely enough the interview had begun with the motion picture *Born to Boogie*, and an analysis of the early seventies passion for films made by famous bands: Slade's *Flame*, David Essex in *That'll Be the Day* and the Gary Glitter semi-tongue-in-cheek documentary, *Remember Me This Way*.

'I always wanted to be an actor,' Mickey begins with a half-serious expression trying to edge out the smile on his face. 'I'm still a frustrated actor which is why I'm always joking. I feel very comfortable in front of a camera and I found the project easy to get into. To be honest, it was a good movie but it's not what I would have done. I would have approached it differently – it was more fantasy and everything but I think, you know, the kids loved it and it is a lovely bit of history now.'

The discussion soon moved on to the speed at which success arrived after the release of 'Ride a White Swan'. We asked Mickey whether he felt that this was planned in any way, after all he was privy to a great many of Marc's thoughts and was the person closest to Marc, with the exception of June. 'That's a very good question but – do you know what? – the funny thing is, consciously for me at least, I didn't have a target. T.Rex for me was like being on a roller coaster and we were just whizzing through, you know, and we didn't know where we were going, but wherever it was it was good and I was having a good time. Great relationships with everybody and happy. So I don't think it was a conscious target – I don't even think Marc knew. I mean, everything he knew, he told.'

The influences of the early days began to creep into the conversation and at this point we felt that June needed to be mentioned. After all, wasn't Marc's wife, now widow, due some credit for the Marc Bolan of those legendary years? 'June was and still is a lovely lady, first and foremost, and she's a great person. This may sound strange, but I think – well, let me say this – Marc owed a lot to her. She was absolutely brilliant. She kept the whole business together.' Mickey then broke into one of his crafty smiles.

'I can give you one great early example of how good she was, right? Me and Marc were doing these university or pub gigs and they had these big bouncers on the door. Marc used to say to June, "We broke the percentage, go and get the cash," – you see it was all pound notes in those days – and June used to just go in there – other bands having hassles with the management – and come out with the cash in her hands!

'June did all the business, worked out the money and all that, on top of which she would get us to the gigs, keep the car filled with fuel and make all the phone calls. This left Marc totally relaxed and able to write his songs, she took all the worry out of his hands. It was a unique relationship, there are few husband and wife partnerships that cross over into business, but theirs did.'

By this stage of the interview Mickey was opening up in great big smiles, the memories that had lain dormant for so many years starting to flood back. We began discussing the ways in which Mickey got his relaxation on tour and how he spent his spare time? 'Well, first you must get a dictionary for me and show me what relaxation means! Because I had no conception of the thing, you know. I used to lie in hotel rooms and count the light fittings after the gigs – I really couldn't sleep because I was on such a high after the shows. I couldn't wind down at all and the only time I cooled off was when we were able to take a couple of weeks off – but by the time I had wound down we were back in it again.'

The touring was non-stop at one stage during those legendary years and for Mickey there were favourite places, as well as those he cared not if he ever saw again. 'I'll tell you what,' recalls Mickey, 'the further north we went in England, the more the kids let themselves go. I mean, in the south they were a bit reserved, but the north – Birmingham, Manchester, Glasgow and Newcastle – if I've missed anywhere out I'm very sorry, but they were all great people.'

Overseas and, in particular, Japan, Mickey remembers with affection: 'Oh, Japan was unbelievable. I tell you what, it's the only place where I felt tall! Cos everybody was so small. When we arrived at the airport it was like a scene from the old newsreel footage of the arrival of the Beatles. We needed a real heavy police escort to get out of the airport and the same when getting to the gigs. We had a most incredible experience at one gig in Tokyo – it was actually our second as the

first had sold out. On our way to this second gig we ended up in the basement of a large arena. We started hearing a lot of banging, windows rattling, and we began to joke about how the fans got down there as we were twenty feet below ground.

'"Oh no," said our security officer, "it's an earthquake." We all went white as sheets, then went on stage and did the fastest set ever! We used to do sets of about an hour and three-quarters – we did this one in forty-five minutes it was like George Formby at 78 rpm!'

On the pressures that were building up for Marc Bolan the superstar, Mickey gives a fascinating alternative to the generally accepted view that Marc was driving himself to stay ahead of the opposition coming from Sweet, Slade and Gary Glitter: 'The pressures Marc put himself under had nothing to do with outside influences. I believe that the pressures came from within Marc himself.'

In fact, then, was Mickey saying that Marc was his own victim and that no one was pushing him? 'I used to talk to Marc about things,' Mickey says, nodding his head in agreement. 'He would never have listened to outside influences – that was a good thing about him – but I feel that he had the formula, totally, and that is why, while always wanting to better himself, the records, and I mean this with no disrespect, began to sound alike.'

So this popularly held theory about constantly checking where the other bands were in the charts, checking out release dates, did not apply to Marc at all? 'I don't think it came into it at all to be honest with you.'

So did Marc never care? 'Oh, I don't say he never cared. I think he was conscious because he would hear something and say, "Oh that's a good track", but he didn't dislike a band because they were number one and he wasn't. In fact I believe that when you are so wrapped up in your own scene you don't have time to worry about everyone else.'

Mickey had put the case very strongly that Marc Bolan was very much his own man and supported our view that Marc was totally unique as far as song-writing was concerned. In an era when all the other bands shared the writing credits in one form or another, and where in the case of Sweet the first hit singles were written by the song-writing team, Chinn and Chapman, Marc stood out as a solo writer.

Did Marc ever involve the rest of the band or did he simply play the new song and tell Bill, Mickey and Steve where he wanted everything? 'When we were very, very busy, instead of having lots of rehearsals we used to have one run through, having first heard Marc play the song in its simplest form. This would have been recorded by Marc and he would set up a rough mix at the desk. We would then all sit around and discuss the ideas, perhaps work on two or three different tempos and then Marc would say, "Oh, yeah, I'd like that one" and it sort of worked like that. The emphasis was on how it felt at any one time.'

So Marc was prepared to take on board the bands' comments? 'Yes,' smiles Mickey, 'but it was always Marc who had the final say.' The smile that remained on Mickey's face was begging for a reaction. 'There is an example of what I mean about Marc. I cannot remember which album it was, but Marc was looking for a title and I came up with a crazy one called "Total T.Rex and the Space Cadets". Now, Marc liked it, you know, and I wanted to do two Bisto boys – the cartoon characters from the adverts for the gravy – with my and Marc's faces on the cartoon characters' bodies. Now, as I say Marc really liked that, but because the idea didn't come from his direction or we didn't come up with it together, he knocked it over – you know, knocked it back. I don't say that Marc was an egoist, but he was very much his own man. He did take some things on board, like the end line in "Get It On" was my contribution, and there were others.'

Tony Visconti had crept in and out of the conversation at various points and we felt it an appropriate time to home in on the 'fifth member of T.Rex'. Did Mickey feel that Marc had discarded him, or at least allowed Visconti to leave, far too easily? 'I don't really think it was a case of that. I think they simply grew apart', explained Mickey. 'You know Marc did like to take control of everything – he found it very difficult to delegate. Tony and Marc used to disagree on things, but who doesn't? I do not believe that the split was a conscious thing and, in fact, I feel it had more to do with the real problem of Tony not always being available exactly when and where Marc needed him to be when recording.

'When we were touring, we would grab some recording time – in Japan, for instance. Tony Visconti would not be there with us, and so Marc would produce instead. That is really how it happened.'

So it was purely accidental? 'Well, perhaps, accidentally on purpose!'

As with Bill Legend, we asked Mickey whether there was a time when he felt that the game was not fun anymore? 'I began to feel that Marc was beginning to repeat himself at the tail-end of 1973 – I so wanted him to change a little in direction, try a different approach. I liked most of the things Marc did, but just one album or single, just to take everyone by surprise, it really wouldn't have hurt at all. There just seemed to be this predictability, that you knew – it was a good thing to have a T.Rex sound, but it could have changed the feeling for me. That's when I started to get thinking, started to question myself – "What am I really doing", you know – I'd lost that excitement.'

What about the emotional side of Marc Bolan, the split from June and the emergence on the scene of Gloria Jones? Could the private events surrounding Marc Bolan have detracted from his artistic state of mind? 'Oh, yeah, cos he went through a lot of emotional changes obviously, and his weight got to be embarrassing and the reviews got bad, for his weight, I mean, not his music. I remember him being referred to as a singing chipolata. It hurt Marc badly, I felt for him – I think he took that really bad. He bled a lot, but he was a very good front man – he could front things out – and that's the sign of a good showman.

'Strangely enough, I never read reviews. If someone told me about one in particular, I would glance at it out of interest, but I never really read them.'

As with everyone else, the parting of the ways with Marc has been, for the most part, full of mystery and speculation. 'We were all in Los Angeles and having finished a tour everyone was going home. But I was very indecisive – everyone wanted me to go back home – but I decided, having been left on my own, that I simply wanted to hang out. I wanted to go to a restaurant, go to a bar and have nothing to do with music – I just needed a change. I flew back some time later and I met Marc a few times and it was a very sad time, we just – split.'

The obvious question was whether Mickey regretted not having hung in there and seen the problems through? 'To be honest with myself, which I must be first and foremost, which is important, I must say that I couldn't stay with the situation as it was. It's not because I didn't love him – the scene, the money, obviously, gosh

that's part and parcel of it – I knew what I was doing and I needed the change. Maybe I was burnt out, maybe the problem was me.

'Just before Marc died, he was wanting to go back on the road and called me and wanted me to go with him. He wanted to go back to the roots – now that would have been exciting. If Marc had said to me in '75 when I wanted to split, "Look, we'll do some acoustic things now and again", that would have been a lovely deal to me – to do it that way, you know, get back into the old bongos and the chair, and back to the cross-legged scene.'

The smiles and laughter that spun throughout the interview vanished when the time came to discuss Marc's death. 'It was six o'clock in the morning when my phone rang. It was Chris, my brother, saying "Have you heard?" and I remember just asking, "No?"

'"Marc's dead … speak to you" and the phone went dead. That was the hardest thing I've ever had to face – ever had to deal with – you never want to believe it. I just couldn't believe that guy, with so much talent and energy, you know. Even when we were apart my heart was with him and my spirit was with him. I took it really badly – I'm not really very good at dealing with death anyway.'

Mickey had taken it badly in a way only someone so close to another human being could have done. He disappeared from existence for nearly fourteen years during which time he lived from day to day with very little purpose. He survived, but only just. 'I've got it all into perspective now, I can look back and see just how badly Marc's death shocked me. I truly went off the rails and although I have now got a perspective on the events, it is still a very sad thing for me, personally.'

Suddenly the smile returns: 'You know, I have a lasting memory of Marc from America. Marc had ordered all these new stage clothes and one day they arrived in this big trunk. He was so excited, like a child on its birthday. He opened the trunk and amongst several other items he pulled out a zebra suit and put it on. Suddenly, as he's turning he starts knocking glasses off the tables and he's still turning around. They had left the tail on the suit! Everyone in the room burst out laughing and Marc turned, picked up the tail, put it under his arm, looked at me and said, "Well that's show business" – such panache.'

.   .   .

REFLECTIONS

At 7.30 on the morning of 16 September 1977, June Bolan was stretching across her bed to turn on the radio as the first strains of the news announced that Marc had died in a car crash. Her phone rang and the voice of Ronni, a friend and the wife of Zoot Money, whispered, 'June?'

'I've just heard, I'll talk to you later' was all June could say in response as she put the phone back on its cradle. Although Marc and June had not been together for almost four years, it was, as she said to herself that day, 'the start of a whole 'nother world. I will never marry again, ever.'

As has become evident over time, June Bolan was without doubt the person who kept Marc together in those early, legendary years. Her dedication to the business side of Marc's career allowed him to concentrate on what he most wanted to do, and indeed did best – make music. It was not what June had anticipated for them; in the beginning all she knew was that she was in love. In an interview we did some years ago in 1987 June touched on her role.

'It didn't even occur to me, but it's something I was very good at because I've always worked in that sort of sphere and dealt with all sorts of record people and I was quite articulate and quite knowledgeable and things like that.'

Of this bonding of two young souls, mentally, physically and musically, June talks, further: 'All Marc knew was how to create and play. That's all he wanted to do; he wanted the trappings that came with it, but he didn't want to know how it got there. I mean he'd sign contracts with the world. Before I knew him he'd signed hundreds of pieces of paper just to be given half an hour's recording time or a chance to do a gig. There were hundreds of people who had little percentages from these tacky pieces of paper that his parents had countersigned because he was under age. It took ages to get him out of them because once he started getting places people realized what they had and they would phone up wanting their percentages.

'So I dealt with them, and Marc trusted me and I would go to all of the business meetings, set up schemes and things for him, check all the contracts and then I'd go home and sit down with him and synopsize – because he really did not want to know. He would take one look at a contract and say, "Oh, twenty pages –

Oh, I can't be bothered with all that." I had to pin him down, make him take in the points that mattered, because it was his life.'

June recalls the early days of change and the lasting effect Marc was to have on the seventies' rock scene: 'To be an innovator is a wonderful feeling and to have glitter on your face when nobody in the whole world had ever done it – nobody in a rock 'n' roll sense – the feelings are great. The fame that went with being an innovator was fine, but when Marc started loosing a little of the status and others around him started having hits – like David Bowie and his Ziggy Stardust era, the red hair and the incredibly glamorous looks and the hits that came with it – when Marc was not having quite so many hits, it became troublesome. But then he would sit down and sigh and say, "Well, I suppose if it wasn't for me none of them would be doing it", which has a strong essence of truth in it, because he actually did stick his neck out against all adversity – and it worked.'

At the realization of being famous at last, June laughs as she remembers; 'The first time ... it's actually a wonderful story. We lived in Little Venice, in Clarendon Gardens and we had the top two floors of a nice Georgian house which we rented. We realized he was famous when we spent the whole of the summer of 1971 on our knees crawling across the drawing room because, God forbid we should stand up, the whole street was full of children. The stereo was at one end of the room and the fireplace was at the other end and to do anything in that room – you did it by first getting on your hands and knees.'

If having to crawl across your floor to play records seemed an invasion of privacy, then no longer being able to go out and do the things everyone else does, as is their right, was yet another price to pay. But, how did the fans get to know where Marc and June lived? 'It's inherent of the whole thing really, once you get to that stage, mail gets sent, people find out, the postman has three daughters who have three boyfriends who all go to different schools and suddenly it's there. I remember one night the door bell rang at about two o'clock in the morning and when I answered the door there stood this tiny girl, well, I mean, a thin child of about fifteen years of age. She had a very broad Scottish accent, no shoes, she'd walked, actually run away, from her home in Glasgow to come to Marc's house. I freaked! I brought her in and phoned the police – I had to because all kinds of

things could have happened, she had ten shillings and there she was, quite prepared to sit on the doorstep and wait for Marc for ever. The police arrived and she was returned to what I can only imagine would be extremely worried and angry parents.'

While June was facing the world on a business level, Marc was totally free and relaxed enough to write his songs. 'Marc would be sitting quietly, reading a book or watching television and he would suddenly leap up and say, "Got to go!" and with that he would disappear into this little room that we had as a music room, turn on the TEACS and you'd hear plonk plonk plonk, or whatever. He never wrote the lyrics first, he never wrote words and then tried to fit them to music. He'd suddenly think of a chord sequence or something would occur to him and you'd hear all this chord changing and then suddenly he'd get a pen or pencil – that's how "Ride a White Swan" happened – overnight.'

·   ·   ·

We felt that the last words of this particular chapter and the end of the non-reference section of the book should be left to June Bolan. What she has to say is largely echoed by all of us who each in our own privileged way knew Marc, either as friends, fellow musicians, family or indeed as we, the authors, fervent fans:

'He was my best friend, always, always my best friend.'

7 · Complete UK Discography: 1968–77

UK Singles

RELEASE DATE	TITLE	HIGHEST CHART POSITION
19 November 1965	**THE WIZARD** Beyond the Rising Sun	
3 June 1966	**THE THIRD DEGREE** San Francisco Poet	
March 1967	**HIPPY GUMBO** Misfit	
24 May 1967	**DESDEMONA** Remember Thomas A Becket	Released as John's Children
Unreleased, but a few copies are in circulation	**MIDSUMMER NIGHT'S SCENE** Sara Crazy Child	Released as John's Children
14 July 1967	**COME AND PLAY WITH ME IN THE GARDEN** Sara Crazy Child	Released as John's Children
16 December 1967 The music was written by Marc but it is not known whether he played on it	**GO GO GIRL** Jagged Time Lapse	Released as John's Children
19 April 1968	**DEBORA** Child Star	34
23 August 1968	**ONE INCH ROCK** Salamanda Palaganda	28
14 January 1969	**PEWTER SUITOR** Warlord of the Royal Crocodiles	
25 July 1969	**KING OF THE RUMBLING SPIRES** Do You Remember	44
20 January 1970	**BY THE LIGHT OF A MAGICAL MOON** Find a Little Wood	
August 1970	**OH BABY** Universal Love	Released as Dib Cochrane and the Earwigs

RELEASE DATE	TITLE	HIGHEST CHART POSITION
2 October 1970	**RIDE A WHITE SWAN** Is It Love \ Summertime Blues	2
19 February 1971	**HOT LOVE** Woodland Rock \ King of the Mountain Cometh	1
2 July 1971	**GET IT ON** There Was a Time \ Raw Ramp	1
1 November 1971	**JEEPSTER** Life's a Gas	2
21 January 1972	**TELEGRAM SAM** Cadillac \ Baby Strange	1
24 March 1972	**DEBORA** (Reissue) One Inch Rock \ Woodland Bop \ The Seal of Seasons	7
5 May 1972	**METAL GURU** Thunderwing \ Lady	1
8 September 1972	**CHILDREN OF THE REVOLUTION** Jitterbug Love \ Sunken Rags	2
1 December 1972	**SOLID GOLD EASY ACTION** Born to Boogie	2
2 March 1973	**20th CENTURY BOY** Free Angel	3
1 June 1973	**THE GROOVER** Midnight	4
August 1973	**BLACKJACK** Squint Eyed Mangle	Released as Big Carrot
16 November 1973	**TRUCK ON (TYKE)** Sitting Here	12
26 January 1974	**TEENAGE DREAM** Satisfaction Pony	13
13 July 1974	**LIGHT OF LOVE** Explosive Mouth	22

MARC BOLAN: THE LEGENDARY YEARS

RELEASE DATE	TITLE	HIGHEST CHART POSITION
Summer 1974	**JASPER C DEBUSSY** Hippy Gumbo \ The Perfumed Garden of Gulliver Smith	
1 November 1974	**ZIP GUN BOOGIE** Space Boss	41
21 June 1975	**NEW YORK CITY** Chrome Sitar	15
26 September 1975	**DREAMY LADY** Do You Wanna Dance \ Dock of the Bay	30
21 February 1976	**LONDON BOYS** Solid Baby .	40
5 June 1976	**I LOVE TO BOOGIE** Baby Boomerang	13
17 September 1976	**LASER LOVE** Life's an Elevator	41
14 January 1977	**TO KNOW YOU IS TO LOVE YOU** City Port	
12 March 1977	**THE SOUL OF MY SUIT** All Alone	42
30 May 1977	**DANDY IN THE UNDERWORLD** Groove a Little \ Tame My Tiger	
5 August 1977	**CELEBRATE SUMMER** Ride My Wheels	
5 August 1977	**BOLAN'S BEST PLUS ONE** Ride a White Swan \ The Motivator \ Jeepster \ Demon Queen	

COMPLETE UK DISCOGRAPHY

UK Albums

7 July 1968

My People Were Fair and Had Sky in Their Hair But Now They're Content to Wear Stars on Their Brows
Hot Rod Momma \ Scenescof \ Child Star \ Strange Orchestras \ Château in Virginia Waters \ Dwarfish Trumpet Blues \ Mustang Ford \ Afghan Woman \ Knight \ Graceful Fat Sheba \ Wielder of Words \ Frowning Atahuallpa
HIGHEST CHART POSITION: 15

14 October 1968

Prophets, Seers and Sages, The Angels of the Ages
Deboraarobed \ Stacey Grove \ Wind Quartets \ Conesuala \ Trelawny Lawn \ Aznageel the Mage \ The Friends \ Salamanda Palaganda \ Our Wonderful Brownskin Man \ Oh Harley \ Eastern Spell \ The Travelling Tragition \ Juniper Suction \ Scenescof Dynasty

18 May 1969

Unicorn
Chariots of Silk \ 'pon a Hill \ The Seal of Seasons \ The Throat of Winter \ Cat Black (The Wizard's Hat) \ Stones for Avalon \ She was Born to be My Unicorn \ Like a White Star, Tangled and Far, Tulip, That's What You Are \ Warlord of the Royal Crocodiles \ Evenings of Damask \ The Sea Beasts \ Iscariot \ Nijinsky Hind \ The Pilgrim's Tale \ The Misty Coast of Albany \ Romany Soup
HIGHEST CHART POSITION: 12

22 March 1970

A Beard of Stars
Prelude \ A Daye Laye \ The Woodland Bop \ Fist Heart Mighty Dawn Dart \ Pavilions of Sun \ Organ Blues \ By the Light of a Magical Moon \ Wind Cheetah \ Beard of Stars \ Great Horse \ Dragon's Ear \ Lofty Skies \ Dove \ Elemental Child
HIGHEST CHART POSITION: 21

11 December 1970

T.Rex
Children of Rarn \ Jewel \ The Visit \ Childe \ The Time of Love is Now \ Diamond Meadows \ Root of Star \ Beltane Walk \ Is It Love? \ One Inch Rock \ Summer Deep \ Seagull Woman \ Suneye \ The Wizard \ The Children of Rarn
HIGHEST CHART POSITION: 13

25 March 1971

Flyback: The Best of T.Rex
Debora \ Child Star \ Cat Black (The Wizard's Hat) \ Conesuala \ Strange Orchestras \ Find a Little Wood \ Once Upon the Seas of Abyssinia \ One Inch Rock \ Salamanda Palaganda \ Lofty Skies \ Stacey Grove \ King of the Rumbling Spires \ Blessed Wild Apple Girl \ Elemental Child
HIGHEST CHART POSITION: 21

17 September 1971

Electric Warrior
Mambo Sun \ Cosmic Dancer \ Jeepster \ Monolith \ Lean Woman Blues \ Get It On \ Planet Queen \ Girl \ The Motivator \ Life's a Gas \ Rip Off
HIGHEST CHART POSITION: 1

2 April 1972

My People Were Fair ... \ Prophets ...
Reissued as a double album. For track listings see original releases: 7 July 1968 and 14 October 1968.
HIGHEST CHART POSITION: 1

5 May 1972

Bolan Boogie
Get It On \ Beltane Walk \ King of the Mountain Cometh \ Jewel \ She was Born to be My Unicorn \ Dove \ Woodland Rock \ Ride a White Swan \ Raw Ramp \ Jeepster \ Fist Heart Mighty Dawn Dart \ By the Light of a Magical Moon \ Summertime Blues \ Hot Love
HIGHEST CHART POSITION: 1

23 July 1972

The Slider
Metal Guru \ Mystic Lady \ Rock On \ The Slider \ Baby Boomerang \ Spaceball Ricochet \ Buick McKane \ Telegram Sam \ Rabbit Fighter \ Baby Strange \ Ballrooms of Mars \ Chariot Choogle \ Main Man
HIGHEST CHART POSITION: 4

5 November 1972

Unicorn \ Beard of Stars
Reissued as a double album. For track listings see original releases: 18 May 1969 and 22 March 1970.
HIGHEST CHART POSITION: 44

23 March 1973	**Tanx**
	Tenement Lady \ Rapids \ Mister Mister \ Broken Hearted Blues \ Shock Rock \ Country Honey \ Electric Slim and the Factory Hen \ Mad Donna \ Born to Boogie \ Life is Strange \ The Street and Babe Shadow \ Highway Knees \ Left Hand Luke
	HIGHEST CHART POSITION: 4
27 September 1973	**Great Hits**
	Telegram Sam \ Jitterbug Love \ Lady \ Metal Guru \ Thunderwing \ Sunken Rags \ Solid Gold Easy Action \ 20th Century Boy \ Midnight \ The Slider \ Born to Boogie \ Children of the Revolution \ Shock Rock \ The Groover
	HIGHEST CHART POSITION: 32
1 February 1974	**Zinc Alloy and the Hidden Riders of Tomorrow or A Creamed Cage in August**
	Venus Loon \ Sound Pit \ Explosive Mouth \ Galaxy \ Change \ Nameless Wildness \ Teenage Dream \ Liquid Gang \ Carsmile Smith and the Old One \ You've Got to Jive to Stay Alive – Spanish Midnight \ Interstellar Soul \ Painless Persuasion v the Meathawk Immaculate \ The Avengers (Superbad) \ The Leopards (Featuring Gardenia and the Mighty Slug)
	HIGHEST CHART POSITION: 12
22 June 1974	**The Beginning of Doves (Early Recordings)**
	Jasper C Debussy \ Lunacy's Back \ Beyond the Rising Sun \ Black and White Incident \ Observations \ Eastern Spell \ You Got the Power \ Hippy Gumbo \ Sara Crazy Child \ Rings of Fortune \ Hot Rod Momma \ The Beginning of Doves \ Mustang Ford \ Pictures of Purple People \ One Inch Rock \ Jasmin '49 \ Charlie \ Misty Mist \ Cat Black (The Wizard's Hat) \ Sally Was an Angel
16 February 1975	**Bolan's Zip Gun**
	Light of Love \ Solid Baby \ Precious Star \ Token of My Love \ Space Boss \ Think Zinc \ Till Dawn \ Girl in the Thunderbolt Suit \ I Really Love You Babe \ Golden Belt \ Zip Gun Boogie
31 January 1976	**Futuristic Dragon**
	Futuristic Dragon (Intro) \ Jupiter Liar \ Chrome Sitar \ All Alone \ New York City \ My Little Baby \ Calling All Destroyers \ Theme for a Dragon \ Sensation Boulevard \ Ride My Wheels \ Dreamy Lady \ Dawn Storm \ Casual Agent
11 February 1977	**Dandy in the Underworld**
	Dandy in the Underworld \ Crimson Moon \ Universe \ I'm a Fool for You Girl \ I Love to Boogie \ Visions of Domino \ Jason B Sad \ Groove a Little \ The Soul of My Suit \ Hang Ups \ Pain and Love \ Teen Riot Structure

8 · Top Twenty Singles Profile:
The Legendary Years of 1970–4

RIDE A WHITE SWAN
Release date: 2 October 1970

OCTOBER	3rd	10th	17th	24th	31st
POSITION	–	–	–	47	37

NOVEMBER		7th	14th	21st	28th
POSITION		31	30	15	7

DECEMBER		5th	12th	19th	26th
POSITION		7	6	12	10

JANUARY 1971	2nd	9th	16th	23rd	30th
POSITION	10	4	4	2	4

FEBRUARY		6th	13th	20th	27th
POSITION		7	14	12	26

MARCH		6th	13th	20th	27th
POSITION		38	–	–	–

HOT LOVE
Release date: 19 February 1971

FEBRUARY		6th	13th	20th	27th
POSITION		–	–	–	34

MARCH		6th	13th	20th	27th
POSITION		17	7	1	1

APRIL		3rd	10th	17th	24th
POSITION		1	1	1	1

MAY	1st	8th	15th	22nd	29th
POSITION	2	6	9	17	21

JUNE		5th	12th	19th	26th
POSITION		31	34	48	–

GET IT ON
Release date: 2 July 1971

JULY	3rd	10th	17th	24th	31st
POSITION	–	21	4	1	1

AUGUST		7th	14th	21st	28th
POSITION		1	1	3	4

SEPTEMBER		4th	11th	18th	25th
POSITION		10	13	28	38

OCTOBER	2nd	9th	16th	23rd	30th
POSITION	40	–	–	–	–

JEEPSTER
Release date: 1 November 1971

NOVEMBER		6th	13th	20th	27th
POSITION		–	37	8	2

DECEMBER		4th	11th	18th	25th
POSITION		3	2	2	2

JANUARY 1972	1st	8th	15th	22nd	29th
POSITION	2	3	10	18	29

FEBRUARY		5th	12th	19th	26th
POSITION		34	44	46	–

TELEGRAM SAM
Release date: 21 January 1972

JANUARY	1st	8th	15th	22nd	29th
POSITION	–	–	–	–	3
FEBRUARY		5th	12th	19th	26th
POSITION		1	1	2	2
MARCH		4th	11th	18th	25th
POSITION		14	18	25	36
APRIL	1st	8th	15th	22nd	29th
POSITION	44	47	–	–	–

DEBORA
(reissue)
Release date: 24 March 1972

APRIL	1st	8th	15th	22nd	29th
POSITION	41	27	12	15	7
MAY		6th	13th	20th	27th
POSITION		8	12	16	39
JUNE		3rd	10th	17th	24th
POSITION		47	–	–	–

METAL GURU
Release date: 5 May 1972

MAY		6th	13th	20th	27th
POSITION		–	9	1	1
JUNE		4th	11th	18th	25th
POSITION		1	1	2	4
JULY	2nd	9th	16th	23rd	30th
POSITION	15	22	28	34	42
AUGUST		6th	13th	20th	27th
POSITION		44	46	–	–

CHILDREN OF THE REVOLUTION
Release date: 8 September 1972

SEPTEMBER	2nd	9th	16th	23rd	30th
POSITION	–	–	14	2	2
OCTOBER		7th	14th	21st	28th
POSITION		2	5	10	17
NOVEMBER		4th	11th	18th	25th
POSITION		29	38	47	–

SOLID GOLD EASY ACTION
Release date: 1 December 1972

DECEMBER	2nd	9th	16th	23rd	30th
POSITION	–	8	4	3	3
JANUARY 1973		6th	13th	20th	27th
POSITION		2	3	7	17
FEBRUARY		3rd	10th	17th	24th
POSITION		28	32	41	–

20th CENTURY BOY
Release date: 2 March 1973

MARCH	3rd	10th	17th	24th	31st
POSITION	–	3	3	3	5
APRIL		7th	14th	21st	28th
POSITION		15	17	26	35
MAY		5th	12th	19th	26th
POSITION		39	–	–	–

THE GROOVER

Release date: 1 June 1973

JUNE	2nd	9th	16th	23rd	30th
POSITION	–	–	6	4	5
JULY		7th	14th	21st	28th
POSITION		8	19	29	35
AUGUST		4th	11th	18th	25th
POSITION		47	50	–	–

(WHATEVER HAPPENED TO THE) TEENAGE DREAM

Release date: 26 January 1974

FEBRUARY		2nd	9th	16th	23rd
POSITION		–	18	13	16
MARCH	2nd	9th	16th	23rd	30th
POSITION	21	26	–	–	–

TRUCK ON (TYKE)

Release date: 16 November 1973

NOVEMBER		3rd	10th	17th	24th
POSITION		–	–	–	38
DECEMBER	1st	8th	15th	22nd	29th
POSITION	20	13	14	12	12
JANUARY 1974		5th	12th	19th	26th
POSITION		15	18	22	32
FEBRUARY		2nd	9th	16th	23rd
POSITION		48	–	–	–

9 · Songs' Anthology: A–Z

The purpose of this chapter is to give a simple ready reference of song titles and list whether they were single or album tracks. We have only listed the UK releases, as to undertake a world-wide catalogue would be a volume work in itself. We have only listed the tracks that appeared on compilations when they were previously unreleased or very rare.

TITLE	FORMAT: LP/SINGLE	ARTISTE: SOLO/BAND
A BEARD OF STARS	Beard of Stars LP	Tyrannosaurus Rex
A DAYE LAYE	Beard of Stars LP	Tyrannosaurus Rex
AFGHAN WOMAN	My People Were Fair LP	Tyrannosaurus Rex
ALL ALONE	Futuristic Dragon LP	T.Rex
ALLIGATOR MAN	Rarities Volume One LP	Marc Bolan
ALL MY LOVE	Dance in the Midnight LP	Marc Bolan
ALL OF MY LOVE	Rarities Volume Two LP	Marc Bolan
AUTO MACHINE	Rarities Volume One LP	Marc Bolan
AZNAGEEL THE MAGE	Prophets, Seers and Sages LP	Tyrannosaurus Rex
BABY BOOMERANG	The Slider LP. Also a flip side track	T.Rex
BABY STRANGE	The Slider LP. Also flip side of a single	T.Rex
BALLROOMS OF MARS	The Slider LP	T.Rex
BEGINNING OF DOVES	The Beginning of Doves LP	Marc Bolan
BELTANE WALK	T.Rex LP	T.Rex
BEYOND THE RISING SUN (version one)	Flip side of a single	Marc Bolan
BEYOND THE RISIN' SUN (version two)	The Beginning of Doves LP	Marc Bolan

TITLE	FORMAT: LP/SINGLE	ARTISTE: SOLO/BAND
BILLY SUPER DUPER	**Billy Super Duper LP**	Marc Bolan
BLACK & WHITE INCIDENT (version one)	**The Beginning of Doves LP**	Marc Bolan
BLACK & WHITE INCIDENT (version two)	**Scare Me to Death LP**	Marc Bolan
BLACK JACK	**Instrumental single**	Big Carrot
BLESSED WILD APPLE GIRL	**Best of T.Rex LP**	T.Rex
BOLAN'S BLUES	**Rarities Volume Three LP**	Marc Bolan
BOLAN'S ZIP GUN	**Rarities Volume Three LP**	Marc Bolan
BORN TO BOOGIE	**Tanx LP. Also flip-side single**	T.Rex
BRAIN POLICE	**Dance in the Midnight LP**	Marc Bolan
BROKEN HEARTED BLUES (version one)	**Tanx LP**	T.Rex
BROKEN HEARTED BLUES (version two)	**Rarities Volume One LP**	Marc Bolan
BUICK MACKANE and the BABE SHADOW	**Billy Super Duper LP**	Marc Bolan
BUICK McKANE	**The Slider LP**	T.Rex
BUST MY BALL	**Rarities Volume Three LP**	Marc Bolan
BY THE LIGHT OF A MAGICAL MOON	**Beard of Stars LP. Released as a single**	Tyrannosaurus Rex
CADILLAC	**Flip side of a single**	T.Rex
CALLING ALL DESTROYERS	**Futuristic Dragon LP**	T.Rex
CARSMILE SMITH	**Rarities Volume Two LP**	Marc Bolan
CARSMILE SMITH & THE OLD ONE	**Zinc Alloy LP**	Marc Bolan & T.Rex
CASUAL AGENT	**Futuristic Dragon LP**	T.Rex

TITLE	FORMAT: LP/SINGLE	ARTISTE: SOLO/BAND
CAT BLACK (THE WIZARD'S HAT) version one	Unicorn LP	Tyrannosaurus Rex
CAT BLACK (THE WIZARD'S HAT) version two	The Beginning of Doves LP	Marc Bolan
CAT BLACK (THE WIZARD'S HAT) version three	Scare Me to Death LP	Marc Bolan
CELEBRATE SUMMER	Released as a single	T.Rex
CHANGE	Zinc Alloy LP	Marc Bolan & T.Rex
CHARIOT CHOOGLE	The Slider LP	T.Rex
CHARIOTS OF SILK	Unicorn LP	Tyrannosaurus Rex
CHARLIE (version one)	The Beginning of Doves LP	Marc Bolan
CHARLIE (version two)	Scare Me to Death LP	Marc Bolan
CHÂTEAU IN VIRGINIA WATER	My People Were Fair LP	Tyrannosaurus Rex
CHILD STAR	My People Were Fair LP	Tyrannosaurus Rex
CHILDE	T.Rex LP	T.Rex
CHILDREN OF RARN	T.Rex LP	T.Rex
CHILDREN OF RARN SUITE (version one)	Marc: The Words and Music LP	Marc Bolan
CHILDREN OF RARN SUITE (version two)	Children of Rarn Suite LP	Marc Bolan
CHILDREN OF THE REVOLUTION	Released as a single	T.Rex
CHRISTMAS BOP	Released as a single	Marc Bolan
CHROME SITAR	Futuristic Dragon LP. Also flip side of a single	T.Rex
CITY PORT	Flip side of a single	Marc Bolan & Gloria Jones

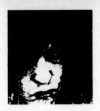

TITLE	FORMAT: LP/SINGLE	ARTISTE: SOLO/BAND
CITY PORT (fast punk)	**Rarities Volume One LP**	Marc Bolan
CONESUALA	**Prophets, Seers and Sages LP**	Tyrannosaurus Rex
COSMIC DANCER	**Electric Warrior LP**	T.Rex
COUNTRY HONEY	**Tanx LP**	T.Rex
CRIMSON MOON	**Dandy In The Underworld LP. Also released as a single**	T.Rex
DANCE IN THE MIDNIGHT	**Dance in the Midnight LP**	Marc Bolan
DANDY IN THE UNDERWORLD (version one)	**Dandy in the Underworld LP**	T.Rex
DANDY IN THE UNDERWORLD (version two)	**Released as a single**	T.Rex
DAWN STORM	**Futuristic Dragon LP**	T.Rex
DEBORA	**Released as a single**	Tyrannosaurus Rex
DEBORAAROBED	**Prophets, Seers and Sages LP**	Tyrannosaurus Rex
DEEP SUMMER	**Released as a single**	Marc Bolan
DEMON QUEEN	**Flip side of a single**	Marc Bolan
DEPTH CHARGE	**Billy Super Duper LP**	Marc Bolan
DESDEMONA	**Released as a single**	John's Children
DESDEMONA (version two)	**Marc: The Words and Music LP**	Marc Bolan\John's Children
DIAMOND MEADOWS	**T.Rex LP**	T.Rex
DOVE	**Beard of Stars LP**	Tyrannosaurus Rex
DO I LOVE THEE	**Dance in the Midnight LP**	Marc Bolan
DOWN HOME LADY	**Dance in the Midnight LP**	Marc Bolan
DOWN HOME LADY (version two)	**Rarities Volume Two LP**	Marc Bolan
DO YOU REMEMBER	**Flip side of a single**	Tyrannosaurus Rex

TITLE	FORMAT: LP/SINGLE	ARTISTE: SOLO/BAND
DRAGON'S EAR	**Beard of Stars LP**	Tyrannosaurus Rex
DREAMY LADY	**Futuristic Dragon LP. Also released as a single**	T.Rex
DWARFISH TRUMPET BLUES	**My People Were Fair LP**	Tyrannosaurus Rex
EASTERN SPELL	**Prophets, Seers and Sages LP**	Tyrannosaurus Rex
ELECTRIC BOOGIE	**Flip side of a single**	T.Rex
ELECTRIC SLIM AND THE FACTORY HEN	**Tanx LP**	T.Rex
ELEMENTAL CHILD	**Beard of Stars LP**	Tyrannosaurus Rex
EVENINGS OF DAMASK	**Unicorn LP**	Tyrannosaurus Rex
EVERYDAY	**Dance in the Midnight LP**	Marc Bolan
EXPLOSIVE MOUTH	**Zinc Alloy LP**	Marc Bolan & T.Rex
FIND A LITTLE WOOD	**Flip side of a single**	Tyrannosaurus Rex
FIST HEART MIGHTY DAWN DART	**Beard of Stars LP**	Tyrannosaurus Rex
FOXY BOY	**Billy Super Duper LP. Also on flip side of a single**	Marc Bolan
FREE ANGEL	**Flip side of a single**	T.Rex
FROWNING ATAHUALLPA (MY INCA LOVE)	**My People Were Fair LP**	Tyrannosaurus Rex
FUTURISTIC DRAGON (Intro.)	**Futuristic Dragon LP**	T.Rex
GALAXY	**Zinc Alloy LP**	Marc Bolan & T.Rex
GET IT ON	**Electric Warrior LP. Also released as a single**	T.Rex
GIRL	**Electric Warrior LP**	T.Rex
GIRL IN THE THUNDERBOLT SUIT	**Bolan's Zip Gun LP**	T.Rex

TITLE	FORMAT: LP/SINGLE	ARTISTE: SOLO/BAND
GOLDEN BELT	**Bolan's Zip Gun LP**	T.Rex
GRACEFUL FAT SHEBA	**My People Were Fair LP**	Tyrannosaurus Rex
GREAT HORSE	**Beard of Stars LP**	Tyrannosaurus Rex
GROOVE A LITTLE	**Dandy in the Underworld LP. Also flip side of a single**	T.Rex
HANG UPS	**Dandy in the Underworld LP**	T.Rex
HIGHWAY KNEES	**Tanx LP**	T.Rex
HIGH WIRE	**Rarities Volume One LP**	Marc Bolan
HIPPY GUMBO	**Released as a single**	Marc Bolan
HIPPY GUMBO (version two)	**The Beginning of Doves LP**	Marc Bolan
HONEY DON'T	**Rarities Volume Three LP**	Marc Bolan
HOPE YOU ENJOY THE SHOW	**Rarities Volume Three LP**	Marc Bolan
HOT GEORGE	**Billy Super Duper LP**	Marc Bolan
HOT LOVE	**Released as a single**	T.Rex
HOT ROD MOMMA	**My People Were Fair LP**	Tyrannosaurus Rex
I BELIEVE	**Rarities Volume Three LP**	Marc Bolan
I LOVE TO BOOGIE	**Dandy in the Underworld LP. Also released as a single**	T.Rex
I'M A FOOL FOR YOU GIRL	**Dandy in the Underworld LP**	T.Rex
I'M COMING TO ROCK 'N' ROLL	**Rarities Volume One LP**	Marc Bolan
I'M WEIRD	**Scare Me to Death LP**	Marc Bolan
INTERSTELLAR SOUL	**Zinc Alloy LP**	Marc Bolan & T.Rex
I REALLY LOVE YOU BABE	**Bolan's Zip Gun LP**	T.Rex
ISCARIOT	**Unicorn LP**	Tyrannosaurus Rex

TITLE	FORMAT: LP/SINGLE	ARTISTE: SOLO/BAND
IS IT LOVE?	**T.Rex LP. Also flip side of a single**	T.Rex
IS IT TRUE?	**Rarities Volume One LP**	Marc Bolan
JASMINE '49	**The Beginning of Doves LP**	Marc Bolan
JASON B. SAD	**Dandy in the Underworld LP. Flip side of a single**	T.Rex
JASPER C. DEBUSSY	**The Beginning of Doves LP**	Marc Bolan
JASPER C. DEBUSSY (version two)	**Released as a single**	Marc Bolan
JEEPSTER	**Electric Warrior LP. Released as a single**	T.Rex
JEWEL	**T.Rex LP**	T.Rex
JITTERBUG LOVE	**Flip side of a single**	T.Rex
JUNIPER SUCTION	**Prophets, Seers and Sages LP**	Tyrannosaurus Rex
JUPITER LIAR	**Bolan's Zip Gun LP**	T.Rex
KING OF THE RUMBLING SPIRES	**Released as a single**	Tyrannosaurus Rex
KNIGHT	**My People Were Fair LP**	Tyrannosaurus Rex
LADY	**Flip side of a single**	T.Rex
LASER LOVE	**Released as a single**	T.Rex
LEAN WOMAN BLUES	**Electric Warrior LP**	T.Rex
LEFT HAND LUKE	**Tanx LP**	T.Rex
LIFE IS STRANGE	**Tanx LP**	T.Rex
LIFE IS STRANGE (version two)	**Rarities Volume One LP**	Marc Bolan
LIFE'S A GAS	**Electric Warrior LP. Also flip side of a single**	T.Rex
LIFE'S AN ELEVATOR	**Flip side of a single**	T.Rex

TITLE	FORMAT: LP/SINGLE	ARTISTE: SOLO/BAND
LIGHT OF LOVE	**Bolan's Zip Gun LP. Also released as a single**	T.Rex
LIKE A WHITE STAR, TANGLED AND FAR, TULIP THAT'S WHAT YOU ARE	**Unicorn LP**	Tyrannosaurus Rex
LIQUID GANG	**Zinc Alloy LP**	Marc Bolan & T.Rex
LIQUID GANG (version two)	**Rarities Volume Two LP**	Marc Bolan
LOCK INTO YOUR LOVE	**Rarities Volume Three LP**	Marc Bolan
LOFTY SKIES	**Beard of Stars LP**	Tyrannosaurus Rex
LONDON BOYS	**Released as a single**	T.Rex
LOVE DRUNK	**Billy Super Duper LP**	Marc Bolan
LUNACY'S BACK	**The Beginning of Doves LP**	Marc Bolan
LUNACY'S BACK (version two)	**Flip side of a single**	Tyrannosaurus Rex
MAGICAL MOON '76	**Flip side of a single**	T.Rex
MAIN MAN	**The Slider LP**	T.Rex
MAMBO SUN	**Electric Warrior LP**	T.Rex
MEADOWS OF THE SEA	**Rarities Volume One LP**	Marc Bolan
MELLOW LOVE	**Billy Super Duper LP. Also released as a single**	Marc Bolan
METAL GURU	**The Slider LP. Also released as a single**	T.Rex
METROPOLIS	**Dance in the Midnight LP**	Marc Bolan
MIDNIGHT	**Flip side of a single**	T.Rex
MIDNIGHT (version two)	**Rarities Volume Two LP**	Marc Bolan
MIDSUMMER'S NIGHT SCENE	**Released as a single (withdrawn)**	John's Children
MISFIT	**Flip side of a single**	Marc Bolan

TITLE	FORMAT: LP/SINGLE	ARTISTE: SOLO/BAND
MISTER, MISTER	**Tanx LP**	T.Rex
MISTER MOTION	**Free 7-inch fan-club single**	Marc Bolan
MISTY MIST	**The Beginning of Doves LP**	Marc Bolan
MONOLITH	**Electric Warrior LP**	T.Rex
MR MOTION	**Rarities Volume One LP**	Marc Bolan
MUSTANG FORD	**My People Were Fair LP**	Tyrannosaurus Rex
MY LITTLE BABY	**Futuristic Dragon LP**	T.Rex
MYSTIC LADY	**The Slider LP**	T.Rex
NAMELESS WILDNESS	**Zinc Alloy LP**	Marc Bolan & T.Rex
NAMELESS WILDNESS (version two)	**Rarities Volume Two LP**	Marc Bolan
NEW YORK CITY	**Futuristic Dragon LP. Also released as a single**	T.Rex
NIJINSKY HIND	**Unicorn LP**	Tyrannosaurus Rex
OBSERVATIONS	**The Beginning of Doves LP**	Marc Bolan
OH, BABY	**Released as a single**	Dib Cochrane and the Earwigs
OH, HARLEY (THE SALTIMBANQUES)	**Prophets, Seers and Sages LP**	Tyrannosaurus Rex
ONCE UPON THE SEAS OF ABYSSINIA	**Best of T.Rex**	T.Rex
ONE INCH ROCK	**Released as a single**	Tyrannosaurus Rex
ONE INCH ROCK (version two)	**T.Rex LP**	T.Rex
ORGAN BLUES	**Beard of Stars LP**	Tyrannosaurus Rex
OUR WONDERFUL BROWN SKIN MAN	**Prophets, Seers and Sages LP**	Tyrannosaurus Rex
OVER THE FLATS	**Rarities Volume One LP**	Marc Bolan

TITLE	FORMAT: LP/SINGLE	ARTISTE: SOLO/BAND
PAIN AND LOVE	Dandy in the Underworld LP	T.Rex
PAINLESS PERSUASION	Rarities Volume Two LP	Marc Bolan
PAINLESS PERSUASION v. THE MEATHAWK IMMACULATE	Zinc Alloy LP	Marc Bolan & T.Rex
PAVILIONS OF SUN	Beard of Stars LP	Tyrannosaurus Rex
PEWTER SUITOR	Released as a single	Tyrannosaurus Rex
PICTURES OF PURPLE PEOPLE	The Beginning of Doves LP	Marc Bolan
PLANET QUEEN	Electric Warrior LP	T.Rex
PLATEAU SKULL	Rarities Volume Three LP	Marc Bolan
'PON A HILL	Unicorn LP	Tyrannosaurus Rex
PRECIOUS STAR	Bolan's Zip Gun LP	T.Rex
PRELUDE	Beard of Stars LP	Tyrannosaurus Rex
RABBIT FIGHTER	The Slider LP	T.Rex
RAPIDS	Tanx LP	T.Rex
RAW RAMP	Flip side of a single	T.Rex
REELIN' AN' A ROCKIN' AN' A BOPPIN' AN' A BOLAN	Rarities Volume Three LP	Marc Bolan
RIDE A WHITE SWAN	Released as a single	T.Rex
RIDE MY WHEELS	Dandy in the Underworld LP. Also flip side of a single	T.Rex
RINGS OF FORTUNE	The Beginning of Doves LP	Marc Bolan
RIP OFF	Electric Warrior LP	T.Rex
ROCK ON	The Slider LP	T.Rex
ROMANY SOUP	Unicorn LP	Tyrannosaurus Rex

TITLE	FORMAT: LP/SINGLE	ARTISTE: SOLO/BAND
ROOT OF STAR	**T.Rex LP**	T.Rex
SAILORS OF THE HIGHWAY	**Across the Airwaves LP**	Marc Bolan
SALAMANDA PALAGANDA	**Prophets, Seers and Sages LP**	Tyrannosaurus Rex
SALLY WAS AN ANGEL	**The Beginning of Doves LP**	Marc Bolan
SAN FRANCISCO POET	**Flip side of a single**	Marc Bolan
SARA CRAZY CHILD	**The Beginning of Doves LP**	Marc Bolan
SARA CRAZY CHILD (version two)	**Flip side track**	John's Children
SATISFACTION PONY	**Flip side track**	Marc Bolan & T.Rex
SATISFACTION PONY (version two)	**Rarities Volume Two LP**	Marc Bolan
SATURATION SYNCOPATION	**Rarities Volume Two LP**	Marc Bolan
SATURDAY NIGHT	**Dance in the Midnight LP**	T.Rex
SATURDAY NIGHT (version two)	**Rarities Volume Two LP**	Marc Bolan
SAVAGE BEETHOVEN	**Rarities Volume Three LP**	Marc Bolan
SCENESCOF	**My People Were Fair LP**	Tyrannosaurus Rex
SCENESCOF DYNASTY	**Prophets, Seers and Sages LP**	Tyrannosaurus Rex
SEAGULL WOMAN	**T.Rex LP**	T.Rex
SENSATION BOULEVARD	**Futuristic Dragon LP**	T.Rex
SHE WAS BORN TO BE MY UNICORN	**Unicorn LP**	Tyrannosaurus Rex
SHOCK ROCK	**Tanx LP**	T.Rex
SHY BOY	**Billy Super Duper LP. Also flip side of a single**	Marc Bolan
SKY CHURCH MUSIC	**Rarities Volume Three LP**	Marc Bolan

TITLE	FORMAT: LP/SINGLE	ARTISTE: SOLO/BAND
SLIDER BLUES	**Rarities Volume One LP**	Marc Bolan
SING ME A SONG	**Marc Shows LP. Also released as a single**	Marc Bolan
SITTING HERE	**Flip side of a single**	T.Rex
SOLID BABY	**Bolan's Zip Gun LP. Also flip side of a single**	T.Rex
SOLID BABY (version two)	**Rarities Volume Three LP**	Marc Bolan
SOLID GOLD EASY ACTION	**Released as a single**	T.Rex
SOUND PIT	**Zinc Alloy LP**	Marc Bolan & T.Rex
SPACEBALL RICOCHET	**The Slider LP**	T.Rex
SPACE BOSS	**Bolan's Zip Gun LP. Also flip side of a single**	T.Rex
STACEY GROVE	**Prophets, Seers and Sages LP**	Tyrannosaurus Rex
STONES FOR AVALON	**Unicorn LP**	Tyrannosaurus Rex
STRANGE ORCHESTRAS	**My People Were Fair LP**	Tyrannosaurus Rex
SUMMER DEEP	**T.Rex LP**	T.Rex
SUNEYE	**T.Rex LP**	T.Rex
SUNKEN RAGS	**Flip side of a single**	T.Rex
SUPERBAD	**Rarities Volume Two LP**	Marc Bolan
SQUINT EYED MANGLE	**Flip side of a single**	Big Carrot
TAME MY TIGER	**Flip side of a single**	T.Rex
TEENAGE DREAM	**Zinc Alloy LP. Released as a single**	Marc Bolan & T.Rex
TEENAGE DREAM: parts one & two	**Rarities Volume Two LP**	Marc Bolan
TEEN RIOT STRUCTURE	**Dandy in the Underworld LP**	T.Rex

TITLE	FORMAT: LP/SINGLE	ARTISTE: SOLO/BAND
TELEGRAM SAM	**The Slider LP. Also released as a single**	T.Rex
TENEMENT LADY	**Tanx LP**	T.Rex
TENEMENT LADY (version two)	**Rarities Volume One LP**	Marc Bolan
THE AVENGERS (SUPERBAD)	**Zinc Alloy LP**	Marc Bolan & T.Rex
THE FRIENDS	**Prophets, Seers and Sages LP**	Tyrannosaurus Rex
THE GROOVER	**Released as a single**	T.Rex
THE KING OF THE MOUNTAIN COMETH	**Flip side of a single**	T.Rex
THE LEOPARDS (FEATURING GARDENIA AND THE MIGHTY SLUG)	**Zinc Alloy LP**	Marc Bolan & T.Rex
THE LILAC HAND OF MENTHOL DAN	**Flip side of a single**	Marc Bolan
THE MISTY COAST OF ALBANY	**Unicorn LP**	Tyrannosaurus Rex
THE MOTIVATOR	**Electric Warrior LP**	T.Rex
THE PERFUMED GARDEN OF GULLIVER SMITH	**Released as a single**	Marc Bolan
THE PILGRIM'S TALE	**Unicorn LP**	Tyrannosaurus Rex
THE SEA BEASTS	**Unicorn LP**	Tyrannosaurus Rex
THE SEAL OF SEASONS	**Unicorn LP. Also flip side of a single**	Tyrannosaurus Rex
THE SLIDER	**The Slider LP**	T.Rex
THE SLIDER (version two)	**Rarities Volume One LP**	Marc Bolan
THE SOUL OF MY SUIT	**Dandy in the Underworld LP. Also released as a single**	T.Rex

TITLE	FORMAT: LP/SINGLE	ARTISTE: SOLO/BAND
THE STREET AND BABE SHADOW	Tanx LP	T.Rex
THE THIRD DEGREE	Released as a single	Marc Bolan
THE THROAT OF WINTER	Unicorn LP	Tyrannosaurus Rex
THE TIME OF LOVE IS NOW	T.Rex LP	T.Rex
THE TRAVELLING TRAGITION	Prophets, Seers and Sages LP	Tyrannosaurus Rex
THE VISIT	T.Rex LP	T.Rex
THE WIZARD	Released as a single	Marc Bolan
THE WIZARD (version two)	T.Rex LP	T.Rex
THE WOODLAND BOP	Beard of Stars LP. Also flip side of a single	Tyrannosaurus Rex
THEME FOR A DRAGON	Futuristic Dragon LP	T.Rex
THERE WAS A TIME	Flip side of a single	T.Rex
THINK ZINC	Bolan's Zip Gun LP. Also released as single	T.Rex
THIS IS MY LIFE	Rarities Volume One LP	Marc Bolan
THUNDERWING	Flip side of a single	T.Rex
TILL DAWN	Bolan's Zip Gun LP	T.Rex
TOKEN OF MY LOVE	Bolan's Zip Gun LP	T.Rex
TRELAWNY LAWN	Prophets, Seers and Sages LP	Tyrannosaurus Rex
T.REX CHRISTMAS RECORD	1972 Fan Club Flexi Disc	T.Rex
TRUCK ON (TYKE)	Released as a single	T.Rex
20th CENTURY BOY	Released as a single	T.Rex
20th CENTURY BABY	Billy Super Duper LP	Marc Bolan
21st CENTURY STANCE	Billy Super Duper LP	Marc Bolan

TITLE	FORMAT: LP/SINGLE	ARTISTE: SOLO/BAND
UNIVERSAL LOVE	**Flip side track**	Dib Cochrane & the Earwigs
UNIVERSE	**Dandy in the Underworld LP**	T.Rex
VENUS LOON	**Zinc Alloy LP**	Marc Bolan & T.Rex
VISIONS OF DOMINO	**Dandy in the Underworld LP**	T.Rex
WARLORD OF THE ROYAL CROCODILES	**Unicorn LP. Also flip side of a single**	Tyrannosaurus Rex
WIELDER OF WORDS	**My People Were Fair LP**	Tyrannosaurus Rex
WIND CHEETAH	**Beard of Stars LP**	Tyrannosaurus Rex
WIND QUARTETS	**Prophets, Seers and Sages LP**	Tyrannosaurus Rex
WOODLAND ROCK	**Flip side of a single**	T.Rex
WORK WITH ME BABY	**Rarities Volume One LP**	Marc Bolan
WRITE ME A SONG (SUPERTUFF)	**Billy Super Duper LP**	Marc Bolan
YOU GOT THE POWER	**The Beginning of Doves LP**	Marc Bolan
YOU'VE GOT TO JIVE TO STAY ALIVE – SPANISH MIDNIGHT	**Zinc Alloy LP**	Marc Bolan & T.Rex
YOU SCARE ME TO DEATH	**Scare Me to Death LP. Also released as a single**	Marc Bolan
ZIP GUN BOOGIE	**Bolan's Zip Gun LP. Released as a single**	T.Rex
11.15 (JAM)	**Rarities Volume Three LP**	Marc Bolan

10 · Diary Dates: 1968–77

1968

APRIL

19 Début Tyrannosaurus Rex single released on the Regal Zonophone label: 'Deborah' catalogue number RZ 3008. Flip-side track 'Childstar' from the first album to be released in July 1968.

MAY

8 First Tyrannosaurus Rex single to enter the British charts.
22 Scotland. First visit by Marc Bolan and Steve Took. Mini tour kicks off in Inverness.
23 Appearance in Motherwell.
24 Dundee.
25 Glasgow.
26 Tour finishes in Edinburgh.

JULY

6 Tyrannosaurus Rex appear among some of the giants of the day at Woburn Abbey Festival. Other acts include Donovan, Family and the Jimi Hendrix Experience.
7 *My People Were Fair and Had Sky in Their Hair, But Now They're Content to Wear Stars on Their Brows*, the first Tyrannosaurus Rex album is released by Regal Zonophone in Mono (LRZ 1005) and Stereo (SLRZ 1005).
27 *My People Were Fair* … album peaks at number fifteen.

AUGUST

23 Second Tyrannosaurus Rex single released by Regal Zonophone. 'One Inch Rock' backed with 'Salamanda Palaganda'. Catalogue number RZ 3011.

OCTOBER

2 Tyrannosaurus Rex tour starts at the Red Lion in Leytonstone, Essex.
9 Albert Hall, Nottingham.
11 King George's Hall, Blackburn.
14 Second Tyrannosaurus Rex album *Prophets, Seers and Sages, The Angels of the Ages* released by Regal Zonophone in Mono (LRZ 1005) and Stereo (SLRZ 1005). On the same day the band appear at the Town Hall, Birmingham.
15 Sheffield City Hall.
20 Guildhall, Southampton.
29 Civic Hall, Dunstable.
30 The tour finishes at the City Hall, Hull.

1969

JANUARY

13 Tyrannosaurus Rex appear at the Queen Elizabeth Hall in London.
14 Third single 'Pewter Suitor' released by Regal Zonophone, backed with 'Warlord of the Royal Crocodiles'. Catalogue number RZ 3016.

FEBRUARY

15 Tyrannosaurus Rex at Birmingham Town Hall.
16 Fairfield Hall, Croydon.
22 Free Trade Hall, Manchester.
23 Colston Hall, Bristol.

| **MARCH** | 1 | Tyrannosaurus Rex appear at Liverpool at the Philharmonic Hall. |
| | 8 | Dome, Brighton. |

| **MAY** | 18 | Third Tyrannosaurus Rex album *Unicorn* released by Regal Zonophone in Mono (LRZ 1007) and Stereo (SLRZ 1007). |

| **JUNE** | 2 | First book of poetry by Marc Bolan published by Lupus Music. *The Warlock of Love* is available by mail order only at 14s 6d. |
| | 14 | *Unicorn* reaches its highest position in the album charts at number twelve. |

| **JULY** | 25 | Fourth Tyrannosaurus Rex single 'King of the Rumbling Spires' released by Regal Zonophone backed with 'Do You Remember'. Catalogue number RZ 3022. |

| **AUGUST** | | Tyrannosaurus Rex embark on first American tour. |
| | 9 | 'King of the Rumbling Spires' spends its one and only week in the singles chart at number forty-four. |

| **OCTOBER** | | Steve Took leaves Tyrannosaurus Rex and is almost immediately replaced by Mickey Finn. |

NOVEMBER	21	First Tyrannosaurus Rex live gig with the introduction of Mickey Finn at the Free Trade Hall in Manchester.
	22	Liverpool Philharmonic Hall.
	23	City Hall, Newcastle.
	30	Mothers, Birmingham.

| **DECEMBER** | 27 | Fairfield Hall, Croydon. |

1970

| **JANUARY** | 20 | Fifth and final Tyrannosaurus Rex single 'By the Light of the Magical Moon' released on the Regal Zonophone label, backed with 'Find a Little Wood'. Catalogue number RZ 3025. |

FEBRUARY	8	Tyrannosaurus Rex appear in Bridgend, Wales, at the Tree Club.
	13	At the Lyceum in the Strand, London.
	18	Dome, Brighton.

| **MARCH** | 22 | The final Tyrannosaurus Rex album *Beard of Stars* is released on Regal Zonophone with Mickey Finn. Only available in Stereo (SLRZ 1013). |

| **APRIL** | 21 | Appearance by Tyrannosaurus Rex at the London Roundhouse alongside the Pretty Things. |

| **MAY** | 9 | Appearance at Imperial College, London. Tyrannosaurus Rex travel to America for second tour, first taste of life over there by Mickey Finn. |

| **OCTOBER** | 2 | Début single for the newly named T.Rex, 'Ride a White Swan' is backed with 'Is It Love?' and the Eddie Cochran classic 'Summertime Blues'. Regal Zonophone changes its identity to FLY RECORDS and the catalogue number is BUG 1. |

DIARY DATES

9 First tour as T.Rex opens at the Albert Hall in Nottingham, prices for tickets are pegged at 10s (50p).

11 King George's Hall, Blackburn.

14 Birmingham Town Hall.

15 Sheffield City Hall.

20 Guildhall, Southampton.

24 'Ride a White Swan' enters British Top Fifty at number forty-seven.

29 Civic Hall, Dunstable.

30 City Hall, Hull.

31 Imperial College, London.

NOVEMBER

4 T.Rex appear at the Mountford Hall, Liverpool.

9 Colston Hall, Bristol.

12 Oxford Town Hall.

21 'Ride a White Swan' enters British Top Twenty at number fifteen, giving Marc his highest placing in three years of singles releases.

24 T.Rex appear at the Guildford Civic Hall.

27 Bournemouth Winter Gardens.

28 At the Roundhouse, Dagenham, the audience is first introduced to Steve Currie on bass guitar.

DECEMBER

3 First of two nights in Glasgow at Green's Playhouse.

4 Second night in Glasgow.

5 'Ride a White Swan' enters Top Ten at number seven.

7 T.Rex at the Hardrock, Manchester.

11 First T.Rex album *T.Rex* released by FLY RECORDS. Catalogue number HIFLY 2. On the day of release T.Rex appear at Welwyn Garden City.

12 T.Rex at the Cardiff Capitol Theatre.

16 Birmingham Odeon.

18 Devizes, Wiltshire.

19 Big Apple Concert Hall, Status Quo are the support band.

20 T.Rex at the Dome in Brighton.

21 Finish gigging for the year in London at Alexandra Palace.
Announcement is made that Steve Currie (bass guitar) and Bill Legend (drums) are to join T.Rex permanently.

1971

JANUARY

2 T.Rex at Sheffield City Hall.

3 Guildhall, Preston.

4 St George's Hall, Bradford.

7 New Theatre, Oxford.

14 Empire, Liverpool.

15 Stoke on Trent, Nottinghamshire.

16 *T.Rex* album enters chart on the day band play at the King's Hall in Aberystwyth, Wales.

21 T.Rex appear at the Gaumont, Southampton.

25 Lyceum in the Strand, London.

FEBRUARY

4 Fairfield Hall, Croydon.

13 North East London Arts Festival.

14 University of Essex.

15 Civic Hall, Guildford.

16 Town Hall, Birmingham.

17 Dundee University, Scotland.

19 'Hot Love' released on FLY RECORDS. Backed with 'Woodland Rock' and 'The King of the Mountain Cometh'. Catalogue number BUG 6.

20 T.Rex appear at Nottingham University.

MARCH

1 T.Rex start three-date tour of Ireland in Cork.

2 Belfast.

3 Final Irish date in Dublin.

13 T.Rex appear at Lancaster University.

20 On the day that 'Hot Love' registers at number one, Marc's first at the top, the band appear at the Winter Gardens complex in Weston-super-Mare.

25 FLY RECORDS release the controversial *Best of T.Rex* album, featuring all Tyrannosaurus Rex material. Catalogue number is TON 2.

APRIL

T.Rex spend the whole of this month at number one in the British singles chart with 'Hot Love'. The band spend the month in America.

MAY

9 T.Rex begin UK tour at the Winter Gardens in Bournemouth. First signs of Bolan mania when riots set the agenda.

11 Porstmouth Guildhall.

14 Albert Hall, Nottingham.

16 Free Trade Hall, Manchester.

17 City Hall, Sheffield.

19 Civic Hall, Wolverhampton.

20 City Hall, Newcastle.

21 Green's Playhouse, Glasgow.

23 Fairfield Hall, Croydon.

24 Colston Hall, Bristol.

25 De Montford Hall, Leicester.

27 St George's Hall, Bradford.

28 End of first leg of tour at Liverpool's Philharmonic Hall.

JULY

2 'Get It On', backed with 'There Was a Time' and 'Raw Ramp', released on the FLY label. Catalogue number BUG 10.

3 Second leg of tour kicks off at the Odeon, Birmingham.

4 Gliderdome, Boston Starlight, Lincolnshire.

DIARY DATES

9 Lewisham Odeon, London.

17 The Pavilion, Bath.

24 'Get It On' at number one, where it stays for four weeks. Second chart topper in six months.

SEPTEMBER

17 *Electric Warrior* album released by FLY, the last album of the contract Marc has with the label. Catalogue number HIFLY 6.

OCTOBER

9 *Electric Warrior* album débuts in the charts at number two, the highest album chart position yet achieved in Marc's career.

19 T.Rex start another tour of the UK labelled the *Electric Warrior* tour when a gig at Portsmouth Guildhall signals the beginning of a seventeen-date marathon.

20 ABC Theatre, Plymouth.

21 Capitol, Cardiff.

23 City Hall, Sheffield.

24 Fairfield Hall, Croydon.

25 St George's Hall, Bradford.

27 The Dome, Brighton.

29 Green's Playhouse, Glasgow.

30 University of Edinburgh.

31 City Hall, Newcastle.

Marc's contract with FLY records comes to an end.

NOVEMBER

1 FLY records anger Marc Bolan by releasing 'Jeepster' backed with 'Life's a Gas' as a new single. Catalogue number BUG 16.

4 ABC at Stockton, Cleveland.

5 Town Hall, Birmingham.

6 Free Trade Hall, Birmingham.

8 De Montfort Hall, Leicester.

9 ABC, Lincoln.

10 ABC, Wigan.

11 Final appearance of this tour at Liverpool Stadium.

27 'Jeepster' reaches number two in the singles chart where it remains for six weeks.

DECEMBER

T.Rex travel to America for start of three-week tour with Alice Cooper.

18 *Electric Warrior* arrives at number one, the first Bolan album to do so. The album spends eight out of the next ten weeks at number one.

1972

JANUARY

1 Marc Bolan signs a marketing and distribution deal with EMI and announces the formation of his own record label the T.Rex Wax Co.

13 T.Rex are voted the world's number one group of 1971 by the readers of the *New Musical Express*.

15 T.Rex gig at the Starlight Club in Boston, Lincs, as a warm-up for the first major European tour.

21 First T.Rex single on Marc's own label is released. 'Telegram Sam' backed with 'Cadillac' and 'Baby Strante'. Catalogue number T.REX 101.

28 European tour begins in Oslo, Norway.

29 'Telegram Sam' straight into the charts at number three. T.Rex appear in Stockholm, Sweden.

30 Copenhagen, Denmark.

31 Hamburg, Germany.

FEBRUARY

1 Munster, Germany, ends the European tour.

5 'Telegram Sam' is at number one in the UK, where it is to stay for two weeks.

11 T.Rex begin tour of America appearing in Seattle, followed by dates in Los Angeles, Boston, Chicago, Detroit, Philadelphia and Cleveland.

27 American tour finishes at Carnegie Hall, New York.

MARCH

18 T.Rex appear at the Empire Pool Wembley for afternoon and evening shows, playing to over 20,000 fans. The concerts are filmed by Ringo Starr.

24 FLY evoke the wrath of Bolan by reissuing 'Debora' along with three other tracks, 'One Inch Rock', 'Woodland Bop' and 'The Seal of Seasons'. Catalogue number ECHO 102.

APRIL

2 FLY reissue *My People Were Fair and Had Sky in Their Hair But Now They're Content to Wear Stars on Their Brows* and *Prophets, Seers and Sages, The Angels of the Ages* as a double package. Catalogue number TOOFA 3/4.

29 On the same day that the single 'Debora' reaches its highest position of number seven in the singles chart, the double pack *My People/Prophets* débuts in the album charts at number two.

MAY

5 Marc releases 'Metal Guru' single, backed with 'Thunderwing' and 'Lady', catalogue number, MARC 1. FLY release a compilation album on the same day entitled 'Bolan Boogie', catalogue number, HIFLY 8.

6 *My People/Prophets* is number one in the album charts.

20 'Metal Guru' sits at number one. It is Bolan's fourth number-one hit of his career. The single keeps the top spot for a total of four weeks.

JUNE

9 Short summer tour starts at the Odeon, Birmingham.

10 Capital Theatre, Cardiff.

16 Belle Vue, Manchester.

19 Marc Bolan is invited to open the new EMI pressing plant in Hayes, Middlesex.

22 A high court writ is issued by Marc against Track Records as, against his wishes, Track plan to issue an album of twenty demos from his pre-Tyrannosaurus Rex days. It was to be titled *Hard on Love*. Track agree to withdraw the planned release.

24 City Hall, Newcastle ends the summer excursion.

JULY

23 *The Slider* album is released by the T.Rex Wax Co. The début album on Marc's own label, it is distributed by EMI and sells over 100,000 copies on day one. Catalogue number BLN 5001.

AUGUST

5 *The Slider* débuts at number four in the UK album charts, the highest position it was to achieve.

SEPTEMBER   **7** T.Rex travel to Canada where they appear at Pierre Fondes Arena, Montreal.

    8 Third T.Rex single of the year 'Children of the Revolution' backed with 'Jitterbug Love' and 'Sunken Rags'. Catalogue number MARC 2.

    14 T.Rex appear at the Academy of Music, New York.

    16 'Children of the Revolution' arrives in the singles chart at number fourteen.

    23 'Children of the Revolution' moves up to number two, it becomes Marc's first single not to top the charts since 'Jeepster' the previous year. It holds the number two spot for three weeks.

NOVEMBER   **5** *Unicorn* and *Beard of Stars* released by FLY as a double package. Catalogue number TOOFA 9/10.

    28 T.Rex appear in Tokyo at start of mini tour of Far East and Australasia.

DECEMBER   **1** T.Rex Wax Co release fourth single of 1972 'Solid Gold Easy Action' backed with 'Born to Boogie', catalogue number MARC 3. This is the first T.Rex single to have only one flip-side track. The beginning of 'Born to Boogie' contains a Christmas message to the fans.

    9 'Solid Gold Easy Action' enters singles chart at number eight. *Unicorn/Beard of Stars* peaks at number forty-four in the album charts.

    14 Première of the motion picture *Born to Boogie* at Oscar One, Brewer Street, London.

    22 T.Rex appear at the Edmonton Sundown, London for the first of three Christmas specials.

    23 Two performances at the Sundown, Brixton, London. It heralds the last time the four-piece T.Rex appear in England and it will be over a year before Marc Bolan gigs in England again.

    31 *Born to Boogie*, the motion picture, opens in London at Hammersmith, Croydon, Romford, Waltham Cross, Catford and Wimbledon.

1973

JANUARY   **6** 'Solid Gold Easy Action' peaks at number two in the first singles chart of 1973.

FEBRUARY   **13** Start of a new European tour beginning at the Sportpasst in Berlin, Germany.

    16 Second venue at Gruguhaile, Essen, Germany.

    17 Next stop, Planten un Blomen, Hamburg.

    18 Measehalle, Nuremberg.

    19 Vienna, Austria.

    20 Stidhalle in Offenbach, Frankfurt.

    22 Sporthalle Belle Vue in Saarbrücken.

    23 Deutschen Museum, Munich.

    25 VFR-Sporthalle, Annaherm.

MARCH   **2** '20th Century Boy' backed with 'Free Angel' is released. Catalogue number MARC 4.

    12 Touring Europe continues at the Olympia in Paris.

    15 Stockholm, Sweden.

    17 Aarhus, Germany.

    19 Oslo, Norway.

    20 Gothenburg, Sweden and Copenhagen, Denmark.

    22 Odense, Denmark.

23 The T.Rex Wax Co release *Tanx*. Catalogue number BLN 5002.

24 Brussels, Belgium.

31 *Tanx* débuts and peaks at number four in the British album charts where it spends just two weeks, before reversing.

JUNE

2 'The Groover' is the second single release of the year, backed with 'Midnight'. The catalogue number is MARC 5.

16 'The Groover' enters the charts at number six.

23 'The Groover' moves up two places to number four where it peaks and falls away over the following weeks.

JULY

14 T.Rex expands as Marc signs guitarist Jack Green.

20 Six-week tour of America opens at Milwaukee Arena and the bill is shared with Three Dog Night. Other cities covered included, Chicago, Memphis, Detroit, Florida, Kansas, Mississippi, Davenport, Iowa, Nassau, New Haven and New York. The tour ends in Winnipeg, Canada.

27 *T.Rex Great Hits* album released by Marc's record label. Catalogue number BLN 5003.

OCTOBER

T.Rex tour Japan, appearing in Tokyo, Osaka, Nagoya, Hiroshima and Fukuoka.

NOVEMBER

3 Four-date tour of Australia kicks off at the Hordern Pavilion in Sydney.

6 Apollo Stadium, Adelaide.

7 Festival Hall, Melbourne.

10 Tour finishes in Brisbane at the Festival Hall. In England *T.Rex Great Hits* appears in the album charts at number thirty-two, its highest placing.

13 Bill Legend quits T.Rex.

16 'Truck On (Tyke)' with 'Sitting Here' on the flip side is released. Catalogue number MARC 6.

DECEMBER

1 'Truck On (Tyke)' enters the singles chart at number twenty.

22 'Truck On (Tyke)' peaks at a disappointing number twelve.

1974

JANUARY

21 Marc Bolan and T.Rex embark on their first tour in England for over a year and a half when they appear at Newcastle City Hall at the start of the Truck Off tour.

22 Glasgow Apollo.

24 City Hall, Sheffield.

26 First T.Rex single of the year is 'Teenage Dream' backed with 'Satisfaction Pony' and the band billing, for the first time, is Marc Bolan and T.Rex. On the same night, the band appear at the City Hall, Manchester.

27 De Montfort Hall, Leicester.

28 Odeon, Birmingham.

FEBRUARY

1 Bolan releases *Zinc Alloy & the Hidden Riders of Tomorrow or A Creamed Cage in August* album. Catalogue number BLNA 7751.

9	'Teenage Dream' enters the singles chart at number eighteen.
16	'Teenage Dream' peaks at number thirteen.

MARCH	**9**	Announcement is made that Tony Visconti and Marc Bolan have parted company after an association stretching back six years.
	16	*Zinc Alloy* album enters the charts at number fifteen.
	23	*Zinc Alloy* album reaches its highest position at number twelve, the worst album-chart placing in four years.

JUNE	**22**	While Bolan is out of the country, Track Records finally release the album of early demos Marc stopped in 1972. The album is called *The Beginning of Doves*. Catalogue number SELECT 2410–201.

JULY	**5**	'Light of Love' single released backed with 'Explosive Mouth'. Catalogue number MARC 8.
	13	'Light of Love' enters the singles chart at number thirty-four.
	20	'Light of Love' peaks at number twenty-two.

SEPTEMBER	**26**	T.Rex appear in America at the Tower Theatre, Upper Darby, Pennsylvania.
	28	T.Rex appear in Johnstown, Pennsylvania.

OCTOBER	**2**	T.Rex appear at the Joint in the Woods, Parsippany, New Jersey, USA.
		Bolan is taken ill and venues cancelled for the remainder of the month.

NOVEMBER	**1**	In Bolan's absence, his record label release 'Zip Gun Boogie' backed with 'Space Boss'. Catalogue number MARC 9.
	9	T.Rex appear at the Roberts Stadium, Evansville, Indiana, USA.
	11	T.Rex appear at the Agora Club, Cleveland, Ohio, USA.
	15	T.Rex play at the Trenton War Memorial Theatre, Trenton, New Jersey, USA.
	16	T.Rex at the Capitol Theatre, Port Chester, New York, USA. In England 'Zip Gun Boogie' enters the singles chart at number fifty.
	17	American circuit comes to an end at the St Moritz Hotel, New York, USA.
	23	Disastrous news for Bolan when 'Zip Gun Boogie' peaks at number forty-one, the lowest chart placing for a single for over four and a half years.

1975

FEBRUARY	**16**	The T.Rex Wax Co release *Bolan's Zip Gun* album. Catalogue number BLNA 7752.

MARCH	**8**	The music paper, *Record Mirror*, reports that Mickey Finn has left T.Rex.

JUNE	**21**	Bolan decides to release 'New York City' backed with 'Chrome Sitar'. Catalogue number MARC 10.

JULY	**12**	On the day T.Rex, with a new line-up, start a small series of warm-up gigs, prior to embarking on the first major British tour for over eighteen months, at the Palace Lido, Douglas, on the Isle of Man, 'New York City' enters the singles chart at number thirty-nine.
	23	T.Rex appear at Tiffany's Great Yarmouth.

25 T.Rex appear at the Pier Pavilion, Hastings.

26 Gig at the Lees Cliffe Hall, Folkestone.

AUGUST	**9** 'New York City' peaks at number fifteen, giving Bolan his first Top Twenty hit single in seventeen months.
SEPTEMBER	**26** 'Dreamy Lady' single, backed with 'Do You Wanna Dance', originally a hit for Chris Montez, and the Otis Redding classic 'Dock of the Bay'. First non-Bolan compositions recorded by Marc since 'Summertime Blues' in 1970. Band announced on record label as the T.Rex Disco Party. Catalogue number MARC 11.
OCTOBER	**11** 'Dreamy Lady' enters the charts at number forty-one.

1976

JANUARY	**31** T.Rex release their new album *Futuristic Dragon*. Catalogue number BLNA 5004.
FEBRUARY	**5** *Futuristic Dragon* tour begins at Chatham Central Hall.
	6 St Albans City Hall.
	7 Lees Cliffe Hall, Folkestone.
	8 Cliffes Pavilion, Southend.
	12 Floral Hall, Southport.
	13 Palace Theatre, Newark.
	14 Grand Pavilion, Withernsea.
	15 Empire Theatre, Sunderland.
	18 Lyceum, London.
	19 Queensway, Dunstable.
	20 Winter Gardens, Bournemouth.
	21 'London Boys' single released backed with 'Solid Baby'. Catalogue number MARC 13.
	23 Town Hall, Birmingham.
	24 Free Trade Hall, Manchester.
	28 Winter Gardens, New Brighton.
MARCH	**1** Apollo, Glasgow.
	3 Municipal Hall, Falkirk.
	4 Civic Centre, Motherwell.
	6 On the same day as T.Rex gig at the Grand Hall in Kilmarnock, 'London Boys' enters the charts at number forty-nine.
	13 'London Boys' peaks at number forty.
JUNE	**5** T.Rex Wax Co release 'I Love to Boogie' backed with 'Baby Boomerang'. Catalogue number MARC 14.
	19 'I Love to Boogie' enters the charts at number forty-four.

JULY	17 'I Love to Boogie' peaks at number thirteen, Marc's first Top Twenty hit in three attempts.
SEPTEMBER	17 New single 'Laser Love' released, backed with 'Life's an Elevator'. Catalogue number MARC 15.
OCTOBER	2 'Laser Love' enters the singles chart at number forty-seven.
	16 'Laser Love' peaks at number forty-one.
DECEMBER	19 T.Rex appear at the Theatre Royal in Drury Lane, London, for a charity performance.

1977

JANUARY	14 Marc and Gloria Jones release the Phil Spector penned 'To Know Him Is to Love Him' as a duet. The title was changed slightly to 'To Know You Is to Love You', backed with 'City Port' – written by Marc Bolan. Released on the EMI label catalogue number EMI 2572.
FEBRUARY	11 New T.Rex album *Dandy in the Underworld* is released. Catalogue number BLN 5005.
MARCH	10 *Dandy in the Underworld* tour begins at Newcastle City Hall. Punk band the Damned are support.
	11 Manchester Apollo.
	12 T.Rex appear at the Glasgow Apollo. 'Soul of My Suit' single, backed with 'All Alone' is released. Catalogue number MARC 16.
	13 Victoria Hall, Hanley.
	14 Colston Hall, Bristol.
	17 Odeon, Birmingham.
	18 Rainbow Theatre, Finsbury Park, London.
	19 Pavilion, West Runton.
	20 Locarno, Portsmouth ends the tour.
APRIL	2 'Soul of My Suit' enters and peaks in the charts at number forty.
MAY	30 'Dandy in the Underworld' single released backed with 'Groove a Little' and 'Tame My Tiger', the first single with two Bolan-penned flip-side tracks since 'Children of the Revolution' in 1972. Catalogue number MARC 17.
AUGUST	5 Last T.Rex Wax Co single released in Marc's lifetime. 'Celebrate Summer' backed with 'Ride My Wheels'. Catalogue number MARC 18.
	24 First of six Granada TV shows, hosted by Marc Bolan simply titled *Marc*.